The Story of a Con

in the Civil War

David E. Johnston

Alpha Editions

This edition published in 2024

ISBN : 9789362924421

Design and Setting By
Alpha Editions
www.alphaedis.com
Email - info@alphaedis.com

Contents

PREFACE

Some twenty-eight years ago I wrote and published a small book recounting my personal experiences in the Civil War, but this book is long out of print, and the publication exhausted. At the urgent request of some of my old comrades who still survive, and of friends and my own family, I have undertaken the task of rewriting and publishing this story.

As stated in the preface to the former volume, the principal object of this work is to record, largely from memory, and after the lapse of many years (now nearly half a century) since the termination of the war between the states of the Federal Union, the history, conduct, character and deeds of the men who composed Company D, Seventh regiment of Virginia infantry, and the part they bore in that memorable conflict. The chief motive which inspires this undertaking is to give some meager idea of the Confederate soldier in the ranks, and of his individual deeds of heroism, particularly of that patriotic, self-sacrificing, brave company of men with whose fortunes and destiny my own were linked for four long years of blood and carnage, and to whom during that period I was bound by ties stronger than hooks of steel; whose confidence and friendship I fully shared, and as fully reciprocated. To the surviving members of that company, to the widows and children, broken-hearted mothers, and to gray-haired, disconsolate fathers (if such still live) of those who fell amidst the battle and beneath its thunders, or perished from wounds or disease, this work is dedicated. The character of the men who composed that company, and their deeds of valor and heroism, will ever live, and in the hearts of our people will be enshrined the names of the gallant dead as well as of the living, as the champions of constitutional liberty. They will be held in grateful remembrance by their own countrymen, appreciated and recognized by all people of all lands, who admire brave deeds, true courage, and devotion of American soldiers to cause and country. For some of the dates and material I am indebted to comrades. I also found considerable information from letters written by myself during the war to a friend, not in the army, and not subject to military duty, on account of sex; who, as I write, sits by me, having now (February, 1914), for a period of more than forty-six years been the sharer of my joys, burdens and sorrows; whose only brother, George Daniel Pearis, a boy of seventeen years, and a member of Bryan's Virginia battery, fell mortally wounded in the battle of Cloyd's Farm, May 9, 1864. DAVID E. JOHNSTON.

Portland, Oregon, May, 1914.

INTRODUCTION

The author of this book is my neighbor. He was a Confederate, and I a Union soldier. Virginia born, he worked hard in youth. A country lawyer, a member of the Senate of West Virginia, Representative in Congress, and Circuit Judge, his life has been one of activity and achievement. Blessed with a face and manner which disarm suspicion, inspire confidence and good will, he makes new friends, and retains old ones.

Judge Johnston (having through life practiced the virtues of a good Baptist), is, therefore, morally sound to the core. He has succeeded, not by luck or chance, but because of what he is. Withal, he has cultivated the faculty for hard work; in fact, through life he has liked nothing so well as hard work.

A vast good nature, running easily into jocular talk, with interesting stories, in which he excels, he is able to meet every kind of man in every rank of society, catching with unerring instinct the temper of every individual and company where he is.

He is thoroughly American, and though having traveled extensively in Europe and the East, he is not spoiled with aping foreigners, nor "rattled" by their frivolous accomplishments. He is likewise an experienced writer, being the author of the history of "Middle New River Settlements, and Contiguous Territory," in Virginia and West Virginia, a work of great value, which cost the author years of persistent research. This volume, "The Story of a Confederate Boy," is written from the heart, with all his might, and all his honesty, and is characterized throughout by fertility, sympathy, and magnanimity, in recording his own personal experiences, and what he saw. C. E. CLINE.

Portland, Oregon.

CHAPTER I

As a boy, but little more than fifteen years of age, I heard and learned much of the pre-election news, as well as read newspapers, by which I was impressed with the thought that Mr. Lincoln was a very homely, ugly man, was not at all prepossessing, some of the newspapers caricaturing him as the "Illinois Ape," "Vulgar Joker of Small Caliber," and much other of the same kind of silly rubbish was said and published. Some of the negroes inquired if he was sure enough a black man. They had heard him spoken of as a "Black Republican."

At the election in November, 1860, Mr. Lincoln, the Abolition-Republican candidate, was chosen President, which caused great anxiety and alarm throughout the Southern states—in fact, in other parts of the country. This fear was intensified later by Mr. Lincoln's utterances in his inaugural address, of which more will be said in later chapter.

Late in the Fall of 1860, and in the early Spring of 1861, I was at school on Brush Creek, in the County of Monroe, Virginia, under the preceptorship of Rev. James W. Bennett, a ripe scholar and genial Christian gentleman. I do not think I progressed as rapidly as I might, most probably on account of some things that tended to distract my attention from my studies. Toward the ending of the school there was much talk about secession and war; in fact, it was the theme of every-day conversation. Even the boys in the school talked learnedly about the questions, and were divided in opinion much in the same proportion as their fathers, guardians and neighbors.

As day after day passed and something new was constantly happening, the feeling and excitement became more intense. As the war clouds began to arise and seemingly to overshadow us, the mutterings of the distant thunder could be heard in the angry words of debate and discussion in the councils of the country, and at home among the extreme advocates of secession on the one hand, and those holding extreme views opposed to the principle and policy of secession on the other. This was not confined to the men alone, but, as before stated, the school boys were would-be statesmen, and in Mr. Bennett's school organized a debating society, in which was most frequently discussed the question, "Shall Virginia Secede from the Union?"—the question being generally decided in the negative.

The meetings of the society were frequently attended by some of the men of the neighborhood, and among them were Col. William Chambers, Major Arnett, and Captain Shue. Colonel Chambers was a fierce, bold, determined, and uncompromising Union man, opposed to secession in any and every form or name in which it could be presented, while Major Arnett and Captain Shue were much of the same way of thinking, but more conservative in their utterances. These men and others frequently took part in the debate and sometimes sat as judges.

When I took part in the discussion it was generally on the affirmative, in favor of secession, my sentiments and convictions leading me in that direction, though as a matter of fact my ideas were very crude, as I knew little of the matter, not having at that time attained my sixteenth year. I had only caught from my uncle, Chapman I. Johnston, who had been educated and trained in the State Rights school of politics, some faint ideas of the questions involved in the threatened rupture.

Naturally following my early impressions, I became and was a strong believer in and an advocate of State Rights, and secession, without fair comprehension of what was really meant by the terms. My youthful mind was inspired by the thought that I lived in the South, among a southern people in thought, feeling and sentiment, that their interests were my interests, their assailants and aggressors were equally mine, their country my country,—a land on which fell the rays of a southern sun, and that the dews which moistened the graves of my ancestors fell from a southern sky; and not only this, but the patriotic songs, and the thought of becoming a soldier, with uniform and bright buttons, marching to the sound of martial music, a journey to Richmond, all animated and enthused me and had the greatest tendency to induce and influence me to become a soldier. Grand anticipations! Fearful reality!

When thinking of this, I am reminded of the story of Bill Douthat of our Company, who, after trying the realities of war and soldier life for a part of one year, returned home, and being strictly inquired of as to what war was, what it meant, or how he liked it, answered, "Well, gentlemen, I have seen the elephant; don't want to see him any more." And after having tried it, I think I can truthfully say that Bill expressed fully our views on the subject.

Leaving school about the last days of March or the first days of April, I returned to my uncle's house.

Although Virginia had not yet seceded, there was an abundance of war talk, and some of the people were rapidly coming to the conclusion that war was inevitable, and that the only way the controversy could or would be settled was by resort to arms, an appeal to the King of Battles,—a submission to the arbitrament of the sword.

Volunteer military organizations already existed in various parts of the state; perhaps there was scarcely a county or city in the Commonwealth that did not have at least one organized volunteer company.

Many overzealous persons declared their purpose to unite their fortunes with the states which had already seceded, whatever the course of Virginia might be, and many of these zealots were so much afraid that there would be no war, or none in Virginia, that they hurried south; however, the ardor of at least some of them became somewhat frigid as the war became flagrant, until it is believed it fell below the freezing point, and some of them going over to the enemy; helped stir up the strife, then ran away, and let the other fellows do the fighting.

CHAPTER II

- **Giles County, its Formation and Early Settlers.**

- **Its Geographical Position, Topography and Population in 1860.**

- **State of Political Parties.**

- **Election of Delegate to the Convention.**

Giles County, named for Hon. William B. Giles, once Governor of Virginia, was created in 1806 out of the territory of Montgomery, Tazewell, and Monroe counties; the county town or seat of justice, Pearisburg, being named in honor of Col. George Pearis, a soldier of the American Revolution, who donated to the county the land on which the town is located. Colonel Pearis was a descendent of a French Hugenot, and was born in the State of South Carolina, February 16, 1746. In a battle with the Tories at Shallow Ford of the Yadkin, North Carolina, on the 14th day of October, 1780, he was wounded in the shoulder, which disabled him for further military service, and on reaching Virginia sought shelter with some relations on the New River, at a place since known as Pepper's Ferry.

The settlement of what is now the territory of Giles County began at a period anterior to the American Revolution, perhaps as early as 1755, if not a few years before that date. Among the early settlers of Giles County were the Lybrooks, Snidows, Harmans, Halls, Napiers, McComas', Clays, Pearis', Peters', Hales McKenseys, Chapmans, Frenches, Johnstons, Shumates, Hatfields, Adkins', Hares, Pecks, Hughes', Wilburns, Shannons, and Banes, who were of Scot-Irish, German, Hugenot and English blood, many of them suffering much from Indian incursions.

The population of this county, in 1860, was 6816, of whom 6038 were free white persons. The county is situated in the midst of the great Appalachian chain or range of mountains, distant from Richmond some three hundred miles. Its length, thirty, by a mean width of twenty miles. New River flows through it in a north-west direction, the chief tributaries of which, in Giles County, are the Sinking, Walker's, Wolf, Big Stony, and Little Stony creeks. Its principal mountains, Walker's, Sugar Run, Angel's Rest, Wolf Creek, East River, Peters' and Salt Pond, which are high, rugged, and precipitous. The streams are rapid, and the surface of the country, other than the river and creek bottoms, generally rough and broken, but the soil rich and fertile. The population in 1861 was made up of sturdy, liberty-loving, hardy mountaineers, engaged chiefly in agricultural pursuits, where brave men are bred, accustomed to the chase and the use of firearms, which fitted them for the hardships and privations of soldier life.

Politically, in 1860 and the early part of 1861, the county was fairly evenly divided between the democratic and whig parties, with perhaps a slight preponderance in favor of the democrats, the great body of whom, with the State Rights whigs, being intensely southern in character, but opposed to extreme measures, or hasty action.

In January, 1861, the legislature ordered an election for delegates to a convention to consider the critical condition of the country, said election to be held on the 4th day of February, at which in Giles County Mr. Manilius Chapman was elected over Mr. Charles D. Peck by a small majority. The convention assembled in Richmond on the 13th of February, of which more hereafter.

CHAPTER III

- **What Will Not Be Attempted Herein.**

- **How the Southern People Viewed the Situation.**

- **Virginia as Peace Maker.**

- **The Peace Conference and Its Failure.**

- **Geographical, Territorial Position.**

- **Assembling of the Convention and Its Action.**

- **Mr. Lincoln's Attitude and Call for Troops.**

- **Adoption of the Ordinance of Secession.**

- **Preparations for Defense.**

It is not herein attempted to record the causes which led to the withdrawal of the Southern States from the Federal Compact of Union framed by the Deputies of twelve of the Thirteen Original States, in the City of Philadelphia on the 17th day of September, 1787, afterwards acceded to and ratified by the states acting by and through conventions of the sovereign people of the states entering into and forming the Compact. Neither will it be discussed whether Secession is a violation of the Constitution, nor whether it is or is not prohibited to the states and no power granted or delegated to the Federal agent to prevent it. It seems no longer a practical question, hence no good purpose could be subserved by a discussion thereof. Some of the arguments, however, of the Southern people are reproduced to show how they viewed the question at the period of which I am writing,—especially what Virginia people said and thought on the subject.

In his inaugural address, Mr. Lincoln had declared his purpose to repossess the forts which had been seized by troops of the seceded states, reading to the Virginia Commissioners on April 13th a paper setting forth his views declaring his purpose to coerce the seceded States. By the Southern people this declaration by Mr. Lincoln was construed as a purpose to wage immediate war of subjugation against the South; in fact, no other meaning could be given to what he said.

Many of the Southern states did not want to leave the Union, abhorred war, and especially was this true of Virginia. She therefore hesitated before taking the step which was to separate her from that Union she had contributed so much to create. Virginia, therefore, made overtures to the government at Washington for an amicable and peaceful solution of the questions agitating the country, which, if not adjusted, would soon plunge the nation into the dreadful war to which we were rapidly drifting. Virginia took the lead in the matter of pacification, by a resolution of her legislature passed early in the month of January, 1861, recommending each of the states to appoint commissioners to a convention, the object of which should be "to adjust the present unhappy controversies." This proposition met the approval of President Buchanan. Most of the states, save those which had then seceded, responded by appointing delegates. In pursuance of this call, the convention met in Washington, February 4, 1861, choosing John Tyler of Virginia, chairman of the convention. After some three weeks' deliberation, this "Peace Congress" submitted a number of propositions, amendments to the Constitution. These propositions, together with most, if not all overtures, came to naught, were rejected by the congress and the party then in control of affairs at Washington.

On December 20th the State of South Carolina had seceded from the Union, affirming and claiming that she, with her sister Southern states, could no longer live on equal terms and in peace in that Union and under that Constitution which many of the Northern states did not hesitate to violate whenever it suited their interests; and further insisting that there had been a powerful party organized in the North, upon principles of ambition and fanaticism, whose purpose was to divert the Federal Government from the external, and turn its power upon the internal interests and domestic institutions of the Southern states; that they had thus in the Northern states a party whose avowed object not only threatened the peace but the existence of nearly one-half of the states of the Republic; that this same party in the North proposed to inaugurate a president, at the head of the Army and Navy, with vast powers, not to preside over the common interests and destinies of all the states alike, but upon partisan issues of avowed hostility, with relentless war to be waged upon the rights and peace of half the states of the Union.

This is but a faint picture of what awaited the Southern states, as they saw it, upon the coming into power of a sectional party, with Mr. Lincoln as chief magistrate, whose inaugural address clearly foreshadowed war.

After repeated demands made by South Carolina, and after several ineffectual attempts by negotiation for the surrender of Fort Sumter, and a Federal fleet had sailed and was then off the harbor of Charleston, for the reinforcing and provisioning of the garrison, it is claimed that treachery and duplicity of the Federal government had been used to deceive the state authorities of South Carolina as to the surrender of the fort.

It was therefore decided to reduce the fort; hence, on the 12th day of April, 1861, the bombardment commenced, the news of which fired the Northern heart, notwithstanding the well known principle that it is not always he who strikes the first blow that is the aggressor, but he who by his conduct or act forces that blow to be given. However, the shot had been fired which aroused the whole country to the highest pitch of excitement, with seemingly no way to allay it. The war was on.

Let us return to the Virginia convention which assembled in Richmond February 13th. These were momentous days. This historic body, composed of the ablest and best men from the Commonwealth of Virginia, carefully considered the grave issues involved, the fearful consequences of civil strife. Upon the best authority it is averred that two-thirds of the men composing this convention were opposed to secession, and preferred to remain in the Union.

A committee on Federal Relations was appointed, which, on the 10th day of March, reported fourteen resolutions, as follows: protesting against all interference with slavery; declaring secession to be a right; defining the grounds on which Virginia would feel herself to be justified in exercising that right, namely: the failure to obtain guarantees; the adoption of a warlike policy by the government of the United States, or to reinforce, or recapture the Southern forts. These resolves clearly defined the attitude of Virginia at this critical moment. After serious discussion pro and con, all but the last of these resolves had passed the convention, when the news was received that the bombardment of Fort Sumter had begun.

Virginia was still for peace and the Union, endeavoring by every means within her power to avert the awful calamity of civil war. Her territorial limits were extensive, reaching from the northeast point of North Carolina northwestward nearly five hundred miles to a point within about one hundred miles of Lake Erie, practically separating the eastern from the western states of the Union; hence her geographical position entitled her to and gave her great power and influence toward a settlement of the impending trouble. It was then claimed,—which was no doubt true,—that the Federal Administration was anxious to see her shorn of her power, which in a measure was accomplished by her dismemberment, by the formation of West Virginia out of her territory, and this by the aid of the Federal power.

Virginia's son was foremost in fanning the flames of revolution, leading to the overthrow of British tyranny and the establishment of American independence. Her son had written the Declaration of Independence. Her son had led the Continental armies during the Revolution, and her son was active in the framing and ratification of the Federal Constitution. Virginia had been among the first to suggest and to assist in creating the compact of union.

To the Confederated states and in the spirit of patriotism and confidence in the continuance of good will, she had given to the Union her north-west territory, an empire within itself, out of which six or more states have been formed. She had furnished seven presidents to the Republic.

It was on the 15th day of April that Mr. Lincoln issued his call for seventy-five thousand troops. Virginia's quota, 2400, were to rendezvous at points in Virginia, thus placing armed soldiers in her territory, though still in the Union, her convention a few days previous having refused to secede by a vote of 89 to 45. This act of Mr. Lincoln was construed by our people as an act of war, and without authority, that power being vested in Congress alone.

Thus it will be seen that all the efforts made by Virginia to preserve the Union and peace had been defeated, Mr. Lincoln having pronounced secession unlawful and void. Virginia was a Southern state, in sympathy with her sister states of the South, and could not be induced to make war on them, nor on the Northern states of the Union. The conduct of the Federal Administration had not only forced her out of the Union, but to take sides in the impending crisis. It was not a Southern Confederacy that Virginia sought or her people fought for, but to uphold and maintain the integrity and sovereignty of the state, and this necessarily meant separate government. I am sure at no time did the people of Virginia think of becoming the aggressors upon the rights of the other states of the Federal Union.

The issue was, therefore, squarely presented. Virginia must decide on which side she would stand. "Choose ye this day whom ye will serve," was the alternative. There was no middle ground, no neutral position, no evading the issue. Against her persistent attachment to the Union, the strongest appeals and bitterest denunciations, Virginia remained unmoved.

When her voice and her pleadings were no longer heard, the news of the bombardment of Fort Sumter, and Mr. Lincoln's call for troops, reached the convention, the supreme moment had come. The die was cast. There could be no further hesitation. On April 17th the Ordinance of Secession, amid anguish and tears, was adopted by a vote of 81 to 51.

The call for troops by the President brought an immediate change in the current of public opinion in Virginia from the mountains to the sea.

The Ordinance of Secession was ratified by the people on the 23d day of May by a majority of 96,750 out of a total vote of 161,018.

Virginians having now made their decision to defend themselves and their state, hastened to arms with ardor and a determined spirit of resistance.

CHAPTER IV

- Organization of Volunteer Forces.

- Giles Not Behind Her Sister Counties.

- A Company Organized at Pearisburg, with James H. French as Captain; Eustace Gibson, First Lieutenant; William A. Anderson, Second Lieutenant; and Joel Blackard, Second Junior Lieutenant; Captains James D. Johnston and R. F. Watts on the Committee to Purchase Uniforms, etc.

- The Ladies of the Town and Country.

- In Barracks and on Drill.

- Anecdote.

- Dixie.

- Our March to Wolf Creek.

- Presentation of Bible and Flag.

On learning of the adoption of the Ordinance of Secession by the convention, the country was ablaze with the wildest excitement, and preparations for war began in earnest. Volunteer organizations of troops were forming all over the state. Why and wherefore, may be asked. Not to attack the Federal Government, to fight the Northern states, but only to defend Virginia in the event of invasion by a Northern army. There was at this time in the county, already organized and fairly drilled, the volunteer company of Capt. William Eggleston, of New River White Sulphur Springs. Pearisburg and the region roundabout in the most part received the news of the secession of the state with apparent relief and gladness, and immediately James H. French, Esq., of Pearisburg, a lawyer and staunch, bold Southern man in education, sentiment and feeling, assisted by others, commenced the enlistment of a company of volunteer infantry to serve for the period of twelve months from the date of being mustered into service, believing that war, if it should come, would not last longer than one year. Enlisting men for war was something new; people are always ready to try something new, and as our people were possessed of a martial spirit, this, together with the excitement and enthusiasm of the occasion, made it no difficult matter to enroll a full company in an incredibly short time. Names were readily obtained, among them my own. I had to go with the boys,— my neighbors and schoolmates, little thinking, or in the remotest degree anticipating, the terrible hardships and privations which would have to be endured in the four years which followed. The idea then prevalent among our people was that we were not to be absent a great while; that there would probably be no fighting; that Mr. Lincoln was not really in earnest about attempting to coerce the seceded states, and if he was, a few Southern men would suffice to put to rout the hordes of Yankeedom. If, however, the Northern people were intent upon war, our people were ready to meet them, because thoroughly aroused.

Our people had by this time arrived at the conclusion that war was inevitable; no settlement on peaceable and honorable terms could be had. They had therefore left the Union, which seemed to them the only alternative. Consequently we felt obliged to appeal to the sword for the settlement of questions which statesmanship had failed to solve; yet always willing to make a child's bargain with the Northern people,—"You leave us alone and we will leave you alone." Extravagant utterances and speeches were made as to Southern prowess. It was even said that one Southern man could whip five Yankees; that the old women of the country with corn-cutters could drive a host of Yankees away; but the people who made these assertions knew little of what they were saying, for ere the war had long progressed we found we had our hands full, and it soon became evident that we might like to find someone to help us let go.

The organization of the company which afterwards became Company D, 7th Virginia regiment, took place April 25, 1861. The only contest for office worth relating was for the captaincy, which was between James H. French and Andrew J. Grigsby, and resulted in the election of the former. The following is a complete roster of the company, with dates of enlistment, rank, etc., to be followed later by a tabulated statement of losses in battle, by disease, desertion, discharge, etc.:

ROSTER OF COMPANY D, 7TH VIRGINIA INFANTRY.

Date of enlistment.	Name.	Rank.
1861—April	James H. French	Captain
1861—April	Eustace Gibson	First Lieutenant
1861—April	W. A. Anderson,	Sec. Lieutenant
1861—April	J. Blackard,	Second Jr. Lieutenant
1861—April	Allen C. Pack	First Sergeant
1861—April	John W. Mullins	Second Sergeant

1861—April	Joseph C. Hughes	Third Sergeant
1861—April	Wm. D. Peters	Fourth Sergeant
1861—April	Hamilton J. Hale	Fifth Sergeant
1861—April	Allen L. Fry	First Corporal
1861—April	Elisha M. Stone	Second Corporal
1861—April	T. N. Mustain	Third Corporal
1861—April	John W. Hight	Fourth Corporal
1861—April	David C. Akers	Private
1861—August	George W. Akers	Private
1861—August	William R. Albert	Private
1861—August	Daniel Bish	Private
1861—August	Allen M. Bane	Private
1861—August	Robert H. Bane	Private
1861—April	Joseph E. Bane	Private
1861—August	Jesse Barrett	Private
1861—April	Alexander Bolton	Private
1861—August	Travis Burton	Private
1861—August	William H. Carr	Private
1861—August	James M. Collins	Private
1861—April	John R. Crawford	Private
1863—March	William Crawford	Private
1861—April	James B. Croy	Private
1861—April	James Cole	Private
1865—January	D. E. Dulaney	Private
1861—April	M. J. Dulaney	Private

1861—August	Tim P. Darr	Private
1861—April	John S. Dudley	Private
1861—April	William H. Douthat	Private
1861—April	Thomas Davenport	Private
1861—August	David Davis	Private
1861—April	Elbert S. Eaton	Private
1861—April	Elisha D. East	Private
1861—April	John W. East	Private
1861—April	Joseph Eggleston	Private
1861—April	James H. Eggleston	Private
1861—April	Francis H. Farley	Private
1861—April	William C. Fortner	Private
1861—April	James H. Fortner	Private
1861—April	Jacob Tyler Frazier	Private
1861—April	William Frazier	Private
1861—August	Creed D. Frazier	Private
1861—April	William A. French	Private
1861—April	John S. W. French	Private
1861—August	Andrew J. French	Private
1861—April	James H. Gardner	Private
1861—August	Francis M. Gordon	Private
1861—April	Andrew J. Grigsby	Private
1861—April	Charles A. Hale	Private
1861—April	John A. Hale	Private
1861—April	John D. Hare	Private

1861—April	Isaac Hare	Private
1861—April	James B. Henderson	Private
1861—August	John Henderson	Private
1861—Mar. 1862	Baldwin L. Hoge	Private
1861—April 1861	James Hughes	Private
1861—April	James J. Hurt	Private
1861—April	George W. Hurt	Private
1861—April	John F. Jones	Private
1861—April	Manelius S. Johnston	Private
1861—August	George Johnston	Private
1861—April	David E. Johnston	Private
1861—April	George Knoll	Private
1861—April	Charles N. J. Lee	Private
1861—April	Joseph Lewy	Private
1861—April	Henry Lewy	Private
1861—April	William H. Layton	Private
1861—April	James Lindsey	Private
1861—April	Patrick H. Lefler	Private
1861—August	Anderson Meadows	Private
1861—August	Ballard P. Meadows	Private
1861—April	John Meadows	Private
1861—April	Newton J. Morris	Private
1862—March	Christian Minnich	Private
1861—April	George A. Minnich	Private
1861—April	John H. Minnich	Private

1861—April	Absalom D. Manning	Private
1861—April	Raleigh Merricks	Private
1861—April	Tapley P. Mays	Private
1861—April	John Q. Martin	Private
1861—April	John H. Martin	Private
1861—August	Wiley W. Muncey	Private
1861—August	George C. Mullins	Private
1862—March	James J. Nye	Private
1861—April	John Palmer	Private
1861—August	Charles W. Peck	Private
1861—April	John W. Sarver	Private
1861—April	Demarcus L. Sarver	Private
1861—April	Josephus Southern	Private
1861—April	Samuel B. Shannon	Private
1861—April	Joseph C. Shannon	Private
1861—April	William H. H. Snidow	Private
1861—April	John P. Sublett	Private
1861—April	William T. Sublett	Private
1861—April	Lewis R. Skeens	Private
1861—April	Alexander Skeens	Private
1861—April	Joseph Skeens	Private
1861—April	Amos L. Sumner	Private
1861—August	Thomas J. Stafford	Private
1861—August	William H. Stafford	Private
1863—January	Ralph M. Stafford	Private

1861—April	Andrew J. Thompson	Private
1861—August	Adam Thompson	Private
1861—August	Alonzo Thompson	Private
1861—April	Thomas S. L. Taylor	Private
1861—April	Lee E. Vass	Private
1861—April	Washington R. C. Vass	Private
1861—April	Elijah R. Walker	Private
1861—April	Lewis N. Wiley	Private
1861—April	Gordon L. Wilburn	Private
1861—April	Ballard P. Watts	Private
1861—April	Hugh J. Wilburn	Private
1861—August	William I. Wilburn	Private
1861—April	Edward Z. Yager	Private
1861—April	Thomas J. Young	Private
1861—August	Isaac Young	Private
1861—April	Jesse B. Young	Private

Whole number of enlisted officers and men, 122.

James Harvey French

Upon the company being organized, a committee was appointed by the county court to purchase uniforms and blankets. This committee, which was composed, as now recollected, of Captains James D. Johnston and R. F. Watts, acted promptly, and the materials for the uniforms were soon on hand. The ladies of the town and surrounding country went to work in earnest and with energy to make our outfits. Herculean as was the task, they accomplished it in an incredibly short time, and we soon donned our bright new clothes, with nice brass buttons, and began to think ourselves soldiers in fact. We occupied as barracks the large frame building on the south-east side of the town, the same lately owned and occupied by Capt. James D. Johnston as a residence. While here we usually had daily squad and company drill, conducted by the accomplished Captain W. W. McComas, then a practicing physician, who had been a soldier in the Mexican War, and who, after the departure of our company, raised and organized a company of which he was made captain. He fell at his post in the forefront of the battle of South Mills, North Carolina, April 19, 1862. He, like many others, died too soon for his country's good, and his friends were greatly grieved and distressed over his untimely death.

During the period which elapsed between the organization and departure for Lynchburg, the designated place of rendezvous, and while in barracks, "the boys," as we were wont to call ourselves, played many pranks upon each other, one of which is worth relating. A sham or mock election was held for the election of a fifth Lieutenant, the choice falling on a very credulous member of the company, who, after the announcement of his election, became quite anxious to know what the duties of his office required of him,—which we, also ignorant of military duties, were unable to answer. With his consent, it was agreed to refer the solution of the matter to Lieutenant Anderson, who was always full of wit and humor, ever ready with answer, and always enjoyed a good joke. Upon the arrival of the Lieutenant, the question was promptly referred to him, and without pausing he promptly answered, "His duties are to carry water and catch fleas out of the soldiers' beds." This seemed satisfactory to the newly elected Lieutenant, and doubtless, as was afterwards demonstrated—for he always obeyed orders and did his duty—he would have proceeded to perform his prescribed duties as explained by Lieutenant Anderson, had not some one told him that it was all a joke and a sell.

Early in May we were invited to a dinner prepared for us by the good people living at and near the mouth of Wolf Creek, whither we marched, partook of a bountiful repast, and returned to our barracks. During our stay in barracks at Pearisburg, as before stated, we were frequently drilled by Captain McComas, who attempted to teach us to keep the step and to cheer, or huzzah. The latter was no easy task, for in fact we never did learn uniformity in the "huzzah," but gradually drifted into that wild "rebel yell," as it was called, which so often sent a thrill of horror into the Yankee ranks, and the memory of which brings a cold chill over those fellows yet! "Dixie," "Bonnie Blue Flag" and other patriotic songs, sung by the choir of the company, greatly enthused us, but "Dixie" had more music in it than all others put together, and it has ever been so, even to this good day.

As all people of all lands are more or less fond of "flag worship," it was altogether fit and proper that the company should have a suitable emblem or flag, and the women, always first in every good work, determined to present to the company a flag and a Bible. Both were soon ready, and it was determined to have a formal presentation of each. Miss Mary Woodram, now the widow of Dr. James O'Keiffe, presented the flag, and the pupils of Pearisburg Academy the Bible, which was placed in the custody of Jacob Tyler Frazier, who had been selected as chaplain, the flag being delivered to Joseph Edward Bane, the company's ensign. J. Smoot Dennis, a boy of only seven years of age, a pupil of the school, presented the Bible, in the following little speech:

"The teachers and pupils of Pearisburg Academy beg leave to present this copy of the Holy Scriptures to our magnificent 'Mountain Boomers' as an expression of our confidence in their Christian faith and patriotism."

To which the chaplain responded:

"On behalf of the 'Mountain Boomers' I accept this book, knowing it to be the Word of God. I shall read it with care and diligence, and on all suitable occasions will endeavor to explain and enforce its claims. Should any of our band fall sick in camp, or be wounded on the field, then from the great treasure of its precious promises I will bring balm for the suffering, and point them to Him whose mission to earth was to bind up the broken-hearted and save that which was lost. If the Pale Horse and his Rider should overtake any of us in a distant land, we will rest in hope of the glorious appearing of Him who is the Resurrection and the Life, and with whom we shall be gathered into that land which no foe invades, and where friends are parted no more."

CHAPTER V

- **The Election for the Ratification of the Ordinance of Secession Was Held on the Fourth Thursday of May, the 23d. On That Day Members of the House of Delegates, and Perhaps Other Officers Were to be Elected.**

- **Our Departure.**

- **Lynchburg and to Manassas Junction.**

The total vote (1033) in Giles County was cast in favor of the ratification of the Ordinance of Secession. Captain William Eggleston was elected to the House of Delegates over Dr. John W. Easley by a majority of 234 votes. Our departure for the rendezvous was delayed for the purpose of giving such members of the company as were entitled to vote the opportunity to do so. To avoid delay and to furnish means to carry us to the railway station twenty-one miles away, preparations were made in advance to transport us in wagons.

The day arrived at last. It was a lovely May morning; the sun shone in all his splendor, the birds sang, all nature seemed to smile, and there was nothing to indicate that this should be the last farewell for many noble Giles County boys to home, friends, and loved ones. We seemed to be going on a holiday journey, to return in a few days. But alas! when the time of departure arrived, what a change of scene! The town was being filled with people,— the fathers, mothers, brothers, sisters, wives, relatives, friends and lovers of the men and boys who were starting on the errand of war. Here was a fond and loving mother clinging to her baby boy, weeping, sobbing, praying the Father of all Mercies to protect and preserve the life of her darling child, amidst the fury and storm of battle. There stood the patriotic, gray haired father, the tears trickling down his cheeks, giving to his beloved son words of comfort, begging that he act the man, be brave, do his duty, refrain from bad habits, and to shun all appearance of evil. A loving sister might be seen with her arms around a brother's neck, reminding him of her love and attachment, and her grief and sorrow at parting from one with whom she had been associated from childhood's days, upon whom she had leaned for protection, and upon whom her fondest hopes for the future rested, and whose face she was, in all probability, gazing upon for the last time. Ears were not deaf to the mutual promises and plighted faith of lovers, of what they hoped one day should be realized. Nor were eyes dim to the parting glances and silent tears, for scarcely could be found an eye that was not bathed in tears on this occasion. It was weeping, shaking of hands, "goodbye," and "God bless you;" and thus the scene continued until the long train of wagons drove us away.

On reaching the residence of that hospitable gentleman, Thomas Shannon, ten miles away, we found in his orchard near the spring a long table on which was spread a splendid dinner. After partaking thereof, and resting a short time, we resumed our journey towards Dublin, arriving there at sunset. Assembling near the station, we were addressed by Colonel Pogue and Mr. Frank Wysor, whose speeches were well timed and patriotic, which, together with the good supper furnished us, had the effect to dispel in some degree the gloom and sadness of the morning. At eleven o'clock P.M. we boarded the train for Lynchburg, arriving there at sunrise next morning. With us were Robinson and Hurt, drummer and fifer, who kept us well supplied with music during that long night's ride. Crowded closely in the coaches, unaccustomed to riding on the cars, and sleeping none, we found ourselves on reaching Lynchburg pretty badly used up. Falling into line at the station, we marched up Bridge street to Main, then to a back street above, going into quarters in a tobacco warehouse, where we remained but a day and night; then to the fair grounds, or Camp Davis, as it was called. There we were joined by Captain Eggleston's company, the Mercer company under Captain Richardson, with several companies from the counties of Franklin, Henry, Patrick, Floyd, Montgomery, and Carroll, which later formed the 24th Virginia regiment of infantry, commanded by Colonel, afterwards Lieutenant-General Jubal A. Early, Peter Hairston, Lieut.-Col., and J. P. Hammett as Major. Colonel Early was not in camp with us at Lynchburg and did not join us until we reached Manassas. The camp was in charge of Lieut.-Col. Hairston, a tall, slender, sandy-haired, blue-eyed man, good natured, but, as we then thought, evidently better qualified to manage his farm down in Henry County than a green military force composed of Virginia gentlemen, unused as they were to restrictions or restraints upon their personal liberty, and not to be broken into harness, so to speak, in a few days.

Our quarters were rude plank sheds with inclined rough floors; our bedding not of feathers, but of a little straw and blankets. As no one in the company knew anything of the art of cooking, what little was done as a matter of course was badly done; the cooking vessels consisting of a tin cup, camp kettle, and frying pan. Bread was generally furnished from the bakers' shops of the city, while meat, rice, beans, peas, etc., had to be dumped into a camp kettle and boiled together—so that it requires no strong stretch of the imagination on the part of the reader to realize that we had a real mess. However, "necessity, the mother of invention," compelled us to learn how to cook, and we were right apt scholars.

In a few days after taking up quarters at Camp Davis, there were issued and delivered to us Springfield muskets, bayonets, scabbards, cartridge boxes, but no ammunition. With these muskets we performed quarter guard, the chief objects of which seemed to be to keep the men out of the city, and to give us some knowledge as to the handling of arms. In accomplishing the first named purpose it was vain; the guards had muskets, but no powder and ball, therefore if anyone were desirous of passing the lines into the city, he had only to wait until the sentry turned on his beat to walk away, then glide quickly across the line; but when the sentry did catch a fellow, he usually made him stand at the point of his bayonet, marking time, until the corporal of the guard could answer the call and conduct the prisoner to the guardhouse. Consequently a different remedy was resorted to by the officers, viz.: The frequent call of the roll, by which the absentees were readily ascertained. This had the effect of lessening the practice of going into the city without permission.

We remained in Lynchburg eight days, breaking camp at Camp Davis Friday the 31st day of May, 1861, and departing that evening in freight cars over the Orange and Alexandria Railroad, for Manassas Junction, a distance of one hundred miles or more. After a long, tiresome, all-night ride, we reached Manassas at sunrise on the morning of June 1st, the morning on which occurred, at Fairfax Court House, a skirmish between the Federal and Confederate outposts, in which Capt. John Q. Marr, of Fauquier, was killed and Major Ewell wounded. The Confederate post at Manassas was named "Camp Pickens" in honor of Governor Pickens of South Carolina.

CHAPTER VI

The day, or second day, after arriving at Manassas, began the organization of the 24th Virginia Regiment of Infantry, with companies from the counties of Carroll, Floyd, Montgomery, Henry, Franklin, Patrick, Mercer and Giles, including our company, the regiment numbering about one thousand men. In our company were J. Tyler Frazier, the company Chaplain, Thomas S. Taylor, James B. Henderson, the Eggleston boys, and perhaps others not now recalled, whose custom and habit was not to retire at night until they had held devotional exercises, thanked God for His past mercies and blessings, and asked His care and protection during the night. This they had not failed to do since leaving home. Taps were sounded at nine o'clock, when all lights must be extinguished. One night at Manassas taps sounded while the boys were at their devotions. Colonel Hairston, seeing the light in their tent still burning, had the boys marched to the guard house; but they were soon released.

After two or three days at the Junction, we marched seven or eight miles to Davis' Ford on the Occoquan river, a stream formed by the junction of Cedar Run, Broad Run, and Bull Run, where we went into camp, pitching tents in a field on the right of the road, behind a skirt of pines which lined the northeast bank of the stream. The Occoquan here is small, with high banks. The field where we camped was barren, not even covered with grass. Our beds were mother earth, our rations were cooked in frying pans and camp-kettles, and we had to wash our own clothes, often without soap.

Company drill was our daily avocation, and when well and closely followed was quite irksome, especially in warm, sultry weather. We also performed quarter guard and did picket duty, the latter by detachments from the various companies, under the command of a commissioned officer, arranged by alternate service. The picket post was nearly a mile in advance of the camp, the small stream flowing between.

No one but a soldier can form any proper conception of the feelings and imaginations of a green boy performing his first night's picket duty on the outpost, and in order to give some meager idea of such a situation, the writer will here relate his personal experience during his first night on the outpost.

It must be kept in mind that the private soldier is supposed to be a mere machine, which, if not in working order, may somewhere along the line produce friction. This machine is supposed to know nothing but his duty and obey orders,—the instructions of his superiors. If placed on outpost duty and told that there is nothing in front of him but the enemy, to keep a sharp lookout, and to warn of the approach of danger, he is not expected to ask questions. My time came to go on duty at ten o'clock at night. The night was cloudy and dark, but pleasant. I was placed on the road by which it was supposed the enemy might come, and given the countersign. From ten o'clock to twelve, midnight, was the time I had to remain, unless the enemy captured or ran me away. What a long two hours! The silence was oppressive. I stood peering through the darkness, away a half a mile or more from any human being, so far as I knew, imagining that every noise or bush shaken by the passing breeze was a veritable foe.

The long two hours had nearly passed away, when—hush! in the distance, on the hard beaten road, not two hundred yards away, came the sound of approaching hoof-beats. Yankees, of course! Who else could they be? I had no information that any of our troops were on the road in front of us.

What should I do? To fire before challenging and alarm the camp would be highly improper; to run away without challenging or firing would be an act of cowardice. So, nerving myself as well as I could under the circumstances, remembering the instructions and countersign, I awaited the coming of the party with all the courage I then seemed to possess. Supposing them to have approached to within some fifty yards,—though it was most likely a hundred yards—I challenged the party, and was answered, "Friends, with the countersign." Then the rejoinder, "One of you dismount, come forward and give the countersign," which was quickly done, and the party passed on; and you, gentle reader, may be assured there was one on his first night's picket duty who breathed with more ease. The spell was broken,— thereafter I had less trouble when on the outpost.

A few nights after this occurrence, the soldier on duty at this same post discharged his musket, which aroused the camp nearly a mile away. Such excitement was scarcely ever witnessed. The long roll sounded, officers cried out, "Fall in! Fall in! The enemy is coming!" Had this been true, there is little doubt that in the confusion and darkness of the night there would have been a stampede.

On the 10th of June we struck tents, taking up the line of march for the village of Occoquan, in the direction of the Potomac River. Our march was only about twelve miles,—hot, dry and dusty, through a country scarce of water. Many a scuffle at wells that we passed took place among the men famishing for water. Our march by the route step was rapid, much too rapid for troops unused to marching and carrying guns, accouterments, knapsacks, blankets and canteens, which, together, weighed from fifty to seventy-five pounds, and which, with our heavy, close fitting coats, made the march burdensome and cruel in the extreme; this in part because the commandant refused to halt for rest or to allow the men to get water. About sunset camp was reached, all hands broken down and exhausted. Next day we marched back, our boys in disgust, some of them quoting the King of France, who with fifty thousand men marched up the hill and then marched down again.

On the tramp to Occoquan occurred a difficulty between Lieutenant Hairston and our Lieutenant Gibson, the two high bloods squaring themselves in the road for battle, but the prompt intervention of Major J. P. Hammett of the regiment prevented the trouble, which threatened to involve not only the two officers but their respective companies, and which difficulty was the cause of the transfer of our company from the 24th to the 7th Virginia regiment.

We rested for a few days in camp in a grove of pines not far from Manassas, to which we gave the name of "Camp Tick Grove," from the fact of our being nearly eaten up by the seed-ticks that infest that region. Nothing of interest transpired while in this camp further than that the writer had a small personal difference with a great burly fellow, which but for the timely interference of a comrade might have resulted in somebody getting threshed. It was a trifling affair, soon over and forgotten. Our transfer to the 7th Virginia regiment being duly effected, we left the "camp of terror" and at Camp Wigfall formed a more perfect union with our new regiment, commanded by Colonel James L. Kemper of Madison County; of which regiment Lewis B. Williams of Orange was lieutenant-colonel, and W. T. Patton, of Culpeper, major.

This regiment was formed of ten companies, two from Madison, two from Rappahannock, one from Albemarle, one from Greene, one from Orange, one from Washington, D.C., one from Culpeper, and one from Giles— designated by letters as follows:

- Co. A, Capt. John Welch, Madison County.
- Co. B, Capt. Thos. B. Massie, Rappahannock County.
- Co. C, Capt. John C. Porter, Culpeper County.
- Co. D, Capt. James H. French, Giles County.
- Co. E, Capt. John Taylor, Culpeper and Orange Counties.
- Co. F, Capt. F. M. McMullen, Greene County.
- [1]Co. G, Capt. Austin Walden, Rappahannock County.
- Co. H, Capt. William Cleary, District of Columbia.
- Co. I, Capt. Isaac Winn, Albemarle County.
- Co. K, Capt. William Lovell, Madison County.
- Dr. C. Bruce Morton, Surgeon.
- Rev. Mr. Bocock, Chaplain.
- Rev. Mr. McCarthy, Chaplain.
- Rev. Mr. J. Tyler Frazier, Acting Chaplain.
- Captain Crisler, Quartermaster.
- Captain Graves, Quartermaster.
- Captain J. W. Green, Commissary.

The adjutants who served in the 7th Virginia were:

- Charles C. Flowerree, 1861 to April, 1862.

- E. B. Starke, April, 1862, to June 30, 1862.

- Hugh M. Patton, ——, 1862, to August 30, 1862.

- John H. Parr, September, 1862, to April, 1865.

- Sergeant-Majors:

- George S. Tansill, to June 30, 1862.

- —— Park, to August 30, 1862.

- David E. Johnston, from November, 1862, to April, 1865.[2]

Camp Wigfall was situate on a beautiful upland grass plot, a short distance southeast of Manassas, and not far from Bull Run. Here we spent the time rather pleasantly, engaging in daily company and battalion drill and doing picket duty on two old country roads leading in the direction of Bull Run.

Blondeau, the Frenchman, belonging to Company H, caused quite a stir and excitement one night by firing his gun at an imaginary foe, which turned out to be a cow browsing in the brush near him. The long roll was sounded, the camp aroused, the regiment put into line, but before this was accomplished the camp was in an uproar, one had lost his boots, another his trousers, another his gun, etc. On the companies reaching their positions in regimental line, ten rounds of ammunition were ordered given each man, and non-commissioned officers directed to make the distribution. It was often told of our Corporal Stone that while dealing out ammunition, on the occasion referred to, one of the men remarked to him that he was giving him more than ten caps, to which the Corporal replied in quick, sharp tone, "Oh, it's no time to count caps now!" Of course no one knowing the Corporal attributed his remark to a want of courage, for no cooler, truer, braver man belonged to the company. Such signification as it had was simply that men unused to "war's alarms," aroused from slumber at the dead of night, would, despite themselves, become excited and impatient, and especially so when they momentarily expected the enemy to pounce upon them; but no enemy came. We, however, rested on our arms the remainder of the night; and though no foe appeared, some of the men were credited with having seen some in the distance—on the hills, in the open fields, but on the coming of light they were found to be merely harmless bushes. On such occasions the imagination is naturally fertile.

The camp becoming quiet, we settled down to old habits. Rations were abundant, more thrown away than we consumed. Inaction was not good for us, and numbers of men became sick and were sent to hospital. Our soldiers, like other people, loved to sleep. If their rest was broken or disturbed at night, by picket, quarter guard, duty, or otherwise, they were sure to take a nap the next day, if the flies, of which there were swarms, would allow them to snooze. If they failed to get their nap during the day they were pretty sure to have their nocturnal slumbers disturbed by gnats and mosquitos, especially during the warm nights.

Two members of our company, Samuel B. and Joseph C. Shannon, sons of Thomas Shannon, had with them a negro servant, Bob, as their cook. Bob was noted for his propensity for laughing, and when in a good glee he could be heard half a mile. He was very patriotic, and declared his purpose to go into battle with his young masters; that he could and would fight as well as we, and shoot as many Yankees. In this Bob was in earnest, as he believed; but ere long his courage was to be put to a practical test, for rumors were already afloat in the camp that the enemy was advancing and a battle impending.

The private soldier knows little of what takes place, other than that which comes under his immediate observation. His general was supposed to keep his own counsels, not allowing his left hand to know what he intended to do with his right. Later on, the private soldier of the Civil War became often as wise about what was on hand as his superior.

An order came to cook three days' rations, pack haversacks, and be ready to move at a moment's notice. From this, we knew something was up. Just what, we could not tell; however, we learned that the enemy was advancing, and a battle to be fought. All was now activity and preparation in the camp, and the men in high spirits and ready for the fray.

---

[1]

] This company joined the regiment on the morning of the day of first battle of Manassas.

[2]

I recall the names of some of the officers who came in later as well as men, to wit: Captains W. O. Fry, Thomas Fry, F. McMullen; J. W. Almerid, Thos. Harris, Phil S. Ashby, Thos. G. Popham, Jas. G. Tansill; Lieutenants Porter, Jas. Brown; Sergeants Wm. Aylor, Apperson, Parrott, Billy Fray, H. C. Burrows and Frank Burrows.

CHAPTER VII

- **Breaking Camp at Wigfall.**
- **The March to the Battlefield.**
- **General Beauregard and His Appearance and Advice.**
- **First Cannon Shot.**
- **Battle of Bull Run.**
- **The Advance.**
- **The Charge.**
- **The Wounded.**
- **Isaac Hare and John Q. Martin.**
- **Retreat of the Enemy.**
- **Severe Artillery Duel.**
- **The Dutchman and His Chunk of Fat Bacon.**
- **Casualties.**

Breaking camp at Wigfall Wednesday noon, July 17, the 7th regiment marched in the direction of McLean's ford on Bull Run, halting on the high land nearly a mile from the Run, and going into bivouac, or rather lying down in an uncultivated field, where we rested quietly during the night. Moving next morning a short distance, we halted on an eminence, overlooking Mitchell's, Blackburn's and McLean's fords, and the country beyond, whence about noon we observed clouds of dust to the north. Very soon after this came the sound of brisk skirmish firing, and the roar of cannon from the direction of Mitchell's ford.

The 24th Virginia, 7th Louisiana, and 7th Virginia regiments constituted a brigade commanded by Col. J. A. Early. Longstreet's brigade, holding Mitchell's ford, against which the enemy directed his principal attack, consisted of the 1st, 11th and 17th Virginia regiments.

The 7th Virginia moved towards the firing along a narrow country road and over a field which had been planted in corn, in which field near the road, in charge of a guard, was a Federal prisoner. We eyed him closely, Bob, the colored cook, especially observing him with interest.

At McLean's gate, as we passed, stood General Beauregard, the commander of the Confederate forces,—slim, strong shouldered, five and a half feet high, of swarthy complexion, and lightish mustache. He appeared calm, and collected, saying as we passed, in a quiet, low tone: "Keep cool, men, and fire low; shoot them in the legs."

I am reminded to state here that in the earlier battles of the war I have seen men in their excitement fire their muskets into the air at an angle of probably forty-five degrees, and others so lowering their guns that the ball would strike the ground but a few feet in front of them. This, however, was soon corrected, and the men took good aim.

Lieut. Eustace Gibson

Pushing forward from this point some two hundred yards, we halted on the left of the road under cover of a belt of pines, which sheltered us from the view of the enemy. Soon came the boom of a cannon, the ball whizzing and buzzing over our heads. All eyes turned in the direction of the noise of the ball, which struck the house near where General Beauregard was standing. A second shot came, the ball cutting away an apple tree near the house referred to, causing a team of horses to take fright and run away, as well as the colored man, Bob, who, musket in hand, had halted at the house, and the last seen of him that day he was making rapid speed for Manassas. Bob never expressed any regret for the run he had made, satisfied with his experience. The rattle of musketry in our front made strange music, affecting some of the men very peculiarly, especially John W. East, of our company, who, on account of a severe pain in the region of his stomach, clasped both hands across that locality, becoming almost doubled, which wholly disabled him for the fight.

The order for the advance came, and forward we went along the narrow country road, through the pines, with a wild yell, and at double quick, accompanied by a section of the Washington (Louisiana) artillery, commanded by Lieutenant Squires. Meeting on the way some wounded men of the 1st Virginia regiment, pale and bleeding, had any other than a pleasant and happy effect upon our nervous systems, tending somewhat to dampen the ardor.

Emerging into an open field two hundred yards from Bull Run, by a movement by the right flank, we were in line advancing towards the stream, the banks of which were covered with timber, the opposite bank sloping from the stream, high and precipitous. Within one hundred yards of the stream, from the opposite bank the enemy poured into our ranks, or rather at us, a volley of musketry, which, thanks to his bad marksmanship, went high, doing little or no damage, but causing us, by common impulse, as is usual with soldiers in their first battle, to fall flat on the ground, and down we went. On the side next the enemy, in front of Isaac Hare, was John Q. Martin, who sprang over Ike, leaving him next the enemy. Ike, with a curse and threatening gesture, compelled Martin to resume his former position. The men of the regiment were immediately upon their feet. As they rose, Lieutenant Squires, whose section of artillery had unlimbered immediately in our rear, gave the command, "Fire!" which command, being mistaken by our men for that of our own officer, caused us to let fly, a terrific volley at the enemy in the woods in our front, and this was followed by a rush with fixed bayonets for the stream, behind which the enemy was posted, forcing him to retreat in confusion, leaving his dead and wounded, knapsacks, haversacks, hats and part of his small arms. Reaching the bank of the stream, the regiment lay down, and there followed for more than an hour a fierce artillery duel between the Federal batteries and the Confederate, the latter under Lieutenant Squires, which resulted in the withdrawal of the former. During this bombardment, shell, shot and shrapnel fell around and among us, wounding a few men of the regiment, but all were quiet, and continued to hug the ground. This was about five o'clock in the afternoon.

George Knoll, "Dutchman," as we usually called him, being in his characteristic mood, but hungry, took from his haversack a chunk of fat bacon, stuffing himself while the artillery fire was in progress.

Quiet now reigning, we began to look after the wounded and prepare for spending the night in battle line in front of the enemy, who had retired from our immediate front, but still hovered near by.

The troops engaged on the Confederate side, save the artillery mentioned, were principally the 1st, 11th and 17th Virginia of Longstreet's brigade, with the 7th Virginia of Early's. The losses in Longstreet's regiments, as reported, were: Killed and mortally wounded, 15, and slightly wounded, 53. Of these casualties 40 were of the 1st Virginia. Seven were wounded in the 7th Virginia of Early's brigade, one killed and five wounded of the artillery. In Company D of the 7th regiment Isaac Hare and James H. Gardner were slightly wounded by spent balls. H. C. Burrows of E Company got a musket ball through his hand; a man of B Company had his hand or fingers mangled by a piece of shell.

The Federal force that attacked us was Richardson's brigade, of Tyler's division, consisting of the 1st Massachusetts, 2d and 3d Michigan, and 12th New York regiments; Ayers' battery, and Brackett's cavalry. The Federal loss, as reported, was 19 killed, 38 wounded, and 26 missing.

CHAPTER VIII

- **Night's Experience on Our First Battlefield.**
- **The Dead and Cries of the Wounded.**
- **Occurrences on the Field.**
- **Sunday, July 21.**
- **Shelled by the Enemy.**
- **March to the Field by the Sound of Battle.**
- **The Battle.**
- **Casualties.**
- **The Pursuit.**
- **To the Outposts.**
- **Incidents.**
- **Winter at Centerville.**

Returning to the battle line, we found ourselves groping around in the dark.

Knowing the enemy to be close by, we quietly went to work throwing up temporary breastworks of logs. The cries of the Federal wounded, and the groans of the dying, the occasional volleys of musketry fired by some of our troops at imaginary foes, with the hooting of owls, made the night hideous and weird, deeply impressing the nature of a lot of young Virginia boys reared in Christian homes. The regiment behaved, however, with great coolness during the entire night, encouraged by the example, presence and good conduct of our brave Lieutenant-Colonel Williams, then in command, Colonel Kemper being absent on public service.

With the coming of daylight, the Confederate scouts crossed the Run, brought in the Federal wounded, and quite a number of muskets, knapsacks, blankets, canteens, cartridge boxes, and hats, thrown away or dropped by the enemy in his flight. By an examination of the dead in front of our regiment, it was ascertained that we had fought the 1st Massachusetts regiment.

This action of the 18th was preliminary to the real battle which came on Sunday the 21st, but on different ground, seven or eight miles northwest of the engagement of the 18th as just described. During Friday and Saturday all was quiet, the Confederate line of battle extending from Union Mills to Stone Bridge, several miles in length; the enemy in the meantime keeping up a showing of force, threatening our front at McLean's, Blackburn's and Mitchell's fords, while his main column was moving or preparing to move northwest to strike the Confederate battle line in flank and reverse on its extreme left.

Our regiment remained Friday night and until late Saturday evening at the same place at which it had halted on Thursday; being then relieved by other troops, retired to a pine thicket close by, where we received a bountiful supply of rations, some in boxes from home,—a thing that makes glad the heart of a homesick boy.

On Saturday evening we were joined by Colonel Kemper, the commander of the regiment. At sunrise on Sunday morning, July 21, the enemy's batteries near Blackburn's opened fire, on account of which we marched to the cover of the pines, between McLean's and Blackburn's fords, remaining but a short time. Our regiment, together with the 7th Louisiana, crossed the Run at McLean's ford for the purpose of attacking the enemy's batteries, which were annoying us, occasionally throwing shots into our ranks, without, however, doing any serious damage. It will be recalled by those present that while lying down behind the pines a shot struck near the center of our company, scattering dust and dirt over us.

While getting into battle line, preparatory to assault upon the batteries, an order came to retrace our steps to the cover of the pines. This was near 12 M. By this time we distinctly heard the roar of heavy guns far to our left, and the great Battle of First Manassas was on.

Near one o'clock P.M., we moved by a rapid gait with the head of the column directed northwest, guided by the sound of the battle. The distance from our starting point, McLean's, by the route we marched to the extreme Confederate left, was fully eight miles, which distance was covered in two hours, notwithstanding the scorching rays of the sun, stopping not for rest or water, for want of which we suffered. The three regiments of Colonel Early's brigade, 7th Louisiana, 7th Virginia, and 13th Mississippi, (the latter substituted for 24th Virginia) passed to the extreme Confederate left, reaching there at near 3:20 P.M., finding themselves face to face with the foe at the Chinn house and in open ground.

Approaching the scene of action, a wild cheer was heard, following which a man on horseback at full speed, hatless, face flushed, covered with perspiration and dust, brandishing his sword over his head, and shouting, "Glory! Glory! Glory!" rode rapidly by. In answer to inquiry as to what was the matter, he said, "We have captured Rickett's battery and the day is ours." This was the first glad news we had received, and all were thrilled with new courage. Cheering wildly, the men pressed forward at double quick. Passing in rear and beyond a wood into which Smith's Confederate brigade had just entered, we encountered the fire of the enemy, mostly United States Regulars. The 7th Virginia here formed quickly, the 7th Louisiana and 13th Mississippi forming on the left, thus completing the battle line with three regiments front. Nor had we arrived a moment too soon, for the enemy was pressing our left flank sorely. There they were, in full view on our front, and to the left of us on the higher ground. Here Colonel Early[3] ordered us not to fire, saying that they were our friends: a grievous blunder upon his part, the result of misinformation not easily explained. Captain Massie, whose company was armed with rifles, called out, "Colonel, they may be your friends, but they are none of ours. Fire, men!" and fire they did.

As we formed, the enemy at long range kept up an irregular fire, inflicting upon our men considerable loss in killed and wounded, and all this while we were too far away from them to pay them back in their own coin. As we pushed forward towards the enemy, they retreated pell-mell, we chasing them over the hill towards Bull Run, considerably in advance of the general Confederate battle line forming across a peninsula created by a sharp curve on Bull Run between Stone Bridge and the mouth of Catharpin creek.

Up to this time we had little realization of the utter defeat of the Federal army, the evidence of which we saw a few days after, when, following his line of retreat, we found guns, caissons, muskets, ambulances, spades, picks and knapsacks abandoned in his flight. The only reason seemingly the enemy had for running as he did was because he could not fly.

The casualties in the 7th Virginia for the limited time it was under fire were severe—nine killed and thirty-eight wounded, our Company D losing Joseph E. Bane, a brave and gallant soldier, killed; Robert H. Bane, A. L. Fry, Manelius S. Johnston, Charles N. J. Lee, Henry Lewy, John P. Sublett, and Samuel B. Shannon wounded. The loss of the Confederates in the battle was 387 killed, 1582 wounded, and 13 captured.

The Federal loss was 2896 men, of which 460 were killed, 1124 wounded, and 1312 captured or missing, besides 26 pieces of artillery, 34 caissons and sets of harness, 10 battery wagons and forges, 24 artillery horses, several thousand stand of small arms, many wagons and ambulances, large quantities of army supplies of all kinds.

The Confederate army remained on the field after the battle for two days, amidst a terrific rainstorm; then marching beyond Centerville, six miles to the east, went into camp in a body of woods, where we remained for some weeks; thence moved a short distance beyond Fairfax Court House. Here we laid out our camp and pitched tents, which was barely done when the long roll sounded and we were quickly on the march in the direction of Alexandria and Washington, whither we should have been pushing the day after the battle; for if vigorous pursuit had been made, Washington would have fallen into our hands.

The march referred to took us to Munson's hill; learning on the way that a brisk skirmish between the enemy and some Confederate troops had occurred during the day, which had only ended with the approach of darkness. Halting near Munson's hill, an order was given to load muskets, and again we moved forward. John W. East, from sheer cowardice—constitutional—he could not avoid it—fell at full length in the road. John turned up in camp a few days after, in fair health and clothed in his right mind. The regiment passed on a few hundred yards to the base of the hill, going into camp. The following morning, Company K, together with Company D, under Captain Lovell, on the right and front of the hill had quite a sharp skirmish with the enemy. Next morning, Saturday, August 30, Major Patton, with Companies B and D, advanced to Bailey's Corners, three-quarters of a mile or so, where they engaged in quite a fusillade with a portion of the Second Michigan regiment, in which a lieutenant of B Company was wounded, and one man of the Michigan regiment was mortally wounded.

In a few days after the skirmish just described, we returned to our camp, where we found peace and plenty. Lieutenant W. A. Anderson, who at Camp Wigfall had been detailed to go back home and secure additional men to fill up the loss in the ranks, caused by sickness, had returned with the following men, to wit: George W. Akers, William R. Albert, David Davis, Creed D. Frazier, A. J. French, Francis M. Gordon, John Henderson, George Johnston, P. H. Lefler, Anderson Meadows, Ballard P. Meadows, Winton W. Muncey, George C. Mullins, Charles W. Peck, Thomas J. Stafford, William H. Stafford, Adam Thompson, Alonzo Thompson, William I. Wilburn and Isaac Young.

With the exception of company and regimental drill, some picket duty, and quarter guard, we did little but cook, eat, write letters and sleep. The weather was hot, the water bad; this, with an overabundance of rations, and insufficient exercise—in fact, a life of almost entire inactivity—were the fruitful sources of disease, and many of the men were sick, a number of them finding their way to the hospital; among them, Allen C. Pack, Ed Z. Yager, William Sublett, John Henderson, William Frazier, H. J. Hale, and doubtless others, not now recalled. Frazier, Henderson, Sublett and Hale died, as did Alonzo Thompson, whose deaths and loss were much regretted. Strange, yet true, that many of our strongest men fell victims to disease, while those apparently much weaker stood the service well.

While on picket duty at Fall's Church, a Captain Farley, with smooth face, fair skin and blue eyes, claiming to be—and was—a South Carolinian, and an independent scout, approached our outpost and proposed that some of the men go with him into the timber in front of the picket and run the Yankees out. Our boys regarded this as preposterous, and on went Farley. He had not been in the woods long till firing began, and he soon returned with blood streaming from his ear: he had a close call.

During the months of August and September we served on frequent picket duty at Munson's, Upton's and Mason's hills, and at Annandale. Our lines were fairly well connected. The enemy, not being able to discover by their scouts what we were doing—what movements we were making, or what force we had, resorted to the use of balloons. On one occasion our people fired at a balloon with cannon shot, and down came the balloon. A short while after this, the balloon was up again, when our boys concluded to at least give the man in the basket—Professor Lowe—a scare; so, rigging up the rear gears of a wagon with a stovepipe, ran the improvised artillery to the hilltop, in full view of the aeronaut, pretending to load. The Professor descended quickly, only to appear again at a safer distance.

On one of our tramps to picket we went to Annandale and remained a day or so with Captain Harrison's Goochland Dragoons, which did outpost duty during the day and we at night. We lived largely, while on picket, on green corn, potatoes, and sometimes other vegetables, a relief from fresh beef, bacon and hardtack, the regular diet of camp life.

As the enemy perfected his lines, he became bolder, pressing closer. This led to frequent collisions between the troops on outpost duty. These conflicts were by general orders discouraged, and called petty warfare. Nor were these without their casualties—if not caused by the enemy, sometimes by accident, or mistake—careless handling of firearms in passing through the brush, carrying of arms at a trail and catching the hammers against some obstacle. One such accident is recalled by which a man by the name of Link, of Captain Eggleston's Giles company, lost his life.

Capt. Robert H. Bane

During the sojourn at Fairfax, a detachment under Lieutenant Allen, of the 28th Virginia, was sent to the station on the railway to guard some baggage and stores deposited there. Of this detachment was John R. Crawford, of our company, who for true physical courage, bravery and self-possession, had scarce an equal; indeed, it was often said of him that he knew no fear—did not know what it meant—never dreamed nor imagined what danger was; that he felt as much at ease in the storm of battle as when resting quietly in the camp. The reader doubtless has heard of the "Louisiana Tigers," who in the first battle of Manassas, when closing with the enemy, threw down their muskets and rushed upon the enemy with their bowie-knives. They were a dangerous, blood-thirsty set—at least so reputed. It was two of these same "Tigers" who found Crawford on guard over the baggage and stores above referred to, which they proposed to appropriate. Crawford warned them to stand off and go away. They paid no heed to the warnings, but persisted in their purpose. Crawford then reversed his musket and downed the man nearest to him, who fell trembling and bleeding at his feet; whereupon his companion quickly advanced to his rescue, but Crawford's belligerent attitude caused him to beat a hasty retreat.

The Winter of 1861-1862 was spent at Centerville in camp, our quarters being constructed of log huts with wooden chimneys. The Winter was cold and dreary, and we had some difficulty in keeping a supply of rations, which had to be transported from the junction six miles away by wagons over a road deep in mud and mire.

Owing to the difficulty of distinguishing our Virginia state flag from many flags of other states carried by the enemy in the battle of Manassas, whereby we had been threatened with serious consequences, such as occurred with our own brigade on that field: it became necessary to have a flag uniform in design for all the Confederate army. Such a flag was designed by Colonel Miles, of South Carolina, and presented by General Beauregard to the army. This flag was about twenty-two inches square, the field red, with blue stripes from corner to corner at right angles, with thirteen white stars; and was ever after our battle flag.

Again we were on picket, Crawford on outpost, with instructions to keep a sharp lookout, as the enemy was near, but not to shoot without calling "halt" the usual three times, and if no halt made, to shoot. Shortly after Crawford took post, his cries of "Halt! Halt! Halt!" were heard, and bang! went his gun. The corporal ran to see what was the matter: he found Crawford standing quietly at his post as if nothing had happened—a stray fat hog had wandered to the post and had not halted at Crawford's command, consequently was dead. Crawford's only explanation was, "I obeyed orders." The hog was roasted, with many compliments for Crawford, and all had a feast.

---

[3]

See Colonel Early's Report, Rebellion Records, Series 1, Vol. II, pp. 555-6.

CHAPTER IX

- **Our Daily Duties.**

- **In Camp.**

- **Among the Last Rencounters.**

- **Lieutenant Gibson, Corporal Stone and Others Hold a Council of War and Determine to Advance and Drive McClellan from Arlington Heights.**

- **March to the Outposts.**

- **Graybacks.**

- **Religious Exercises.**

- **Incidents of Camp.**

- **Depletion of the Army.**

- **Re-enlistments and Furloughs.**

- **Retreat from Manassas Behind the Rappahannock.**

- **Albert and Snidow.**

- **Gordonsville.**

Our duties in camp during the Winter were not onerous, save quarter guard in inclement weather, especially rain and extreme cold, for it will be remembered that we had no shelter on quarter guard post—that is, none while on post and on the beat, as a guard must always be in the open, both as to weather and to the foe. The guards were divided into three reliefs: the first went on at 9 o'clock A.M., the second at 11, the third at 1. This order was observed during the twenty-four hours. When off post we were required to remain at the guard house, unless by special permission of the officer of the guard. The quarter guard were supposed to be the special custodians of the quiet and safety of the camp. The mode of placing guard on post was as follows: A sergeant or corporal commenced at the top of the roll, the number of men being equal to the number of posts. Beginning with post number one, we marched around the entire camp, relieving each sentinel with a new man. When this was to be performed at night, the countersign (a pass word adopted at army headquarters and transmitted to the various subordinates) was delivered in a whisper to the guards by the officers thereof, so that as the sergeant with the relief guard approached the sentry, he was required to halt and give the countersign.

Colonel Kemper, still a member of the General Assembly of Virginia, was absent for the greater part of the Winter. Lieutenant-Colonel L. B. Williams, a rigid disciplinarian, who was left in command, endeavored by watchfulness, to have everything done in strict military style; frequently visiting the guard house, having the officer turn out the guard, call the roll, and woe to the man absent or out of line when his name was called. Punishment was sure to follow in the way of double duty or otherwise. On one occasion Lieutenant Anderson and W. H. Layton, having both imbibed too freely, took a jaunt to the guard house, where they had no business, and here Colonel Williams, on one of his visits, found them. Layton was placed in the guard house and the lieutenant in arrest.

During this stay in Winter quarters, Privates Mays, Farley, Thompson and John W. East had an altercation, the last (save two) which occurred in the company. It was not an uncommon thing for the soldiers to discuss the conduct of the war, the remissness and failure of commanders, the probabilities and improbabilities of success, peace, the plan of battles, and the war policy, offensive and defensive. A discussion of this kind is well remembered as having occurred between Lieutenant Gibson, then officer of the day; Corporal Stone, Sergeant Peters, Sarver, Hare and others, in the quarters of my mess, while at Centerville. It was at night; the boys had gotten in a little stimulant. Lieutenant Gibson dropped in, and with the others, imbibing freely, began in a very serious way the discussion of the surest and quickest way or mode of ending the war, and restoring peace to our distracted country. After much discussion pro and con, which lasted practically throughout the night, Corporal Stone submitted a plan to which all readily assented, and which was as follows: To "attack immediately General McClellan's army, drive it from Arlington Heights, capture the Federal capital, then propose an armistice and congress of the states." Stone was for starting that night, for prompt and aggressive action, but Peters favored postponement until morning, which was by this time at hand. Just then the long roll sounded to arms, and a march toward Washington, sure enough, began, but with only our regiment. And, oh! such headaches as Stone, Peters, Gibson and the others in the war council had, and how formidable and impregnable now appeared Arlington, which a few hours before was to them but a mole hill. Our mission was to relieve a Louisiana regiment then on picket near Fairfax, where we remained for a week, occupying the quarters just vacated by the Louisianians. Here it was that we formed our first acquaintance with the "graybacks," which filled our clothing and blankets, much to our discomfort. Oh! the digging under the shirt collar, under the arm pits, and every point where the cruel pest found the flesh of the poor soldier. It was a difficult matter to rid ourselves of them—they seemed over anxious to remain with us. Nothing short of boiling them hard in water got rid of them. The next Summer on the peninsula, in the swamps of the Chickahominy, and around Richmond, we had them in abundance, the boys often saying that they had stamped upon their backs the letters, "I.F.W.," which, interpreted, meant "In for the war."

During our stay in Winter quarters at Centerville, there was little, if any, preaching or religious exercises, as there was no place to have public services, and the weather was too severe to hold services in the open. The mess of J. Tyler Frazier, in which were Thomas S. Taylor, James B. Henderson, F. H. Farley, John F. Jones, William C. Fortner, Joseph Eggleston, James Eggleston, and perhaps others, never neglected their religious duties, and in quarters invariably read a chapter of the Bible, sang a hymn, and prayed before retiring at night. These men, by their upright conduct, observance of their religious duties, their Christian character and conversation, had great influence over their comrades, and especially upon the conduct and morals of the company.

The expiration of the term of service, twelve months, of most of the men was rapidly approaching; the ranks having been much depleted by sickness, death and other causes. No adequate provision had yet been made for the retention of those already in the field, or for the filling of the ranks. It was evident that if the war was to be prolonged, and the contest maintained, we must have an army. With one year's service many were satisfied; the fever had worn off, enthusiasm was on the wane. The government, to induce re-enlistment, was offering fifty dollars bounty and thirty-day furlough. Quite a number availed themselves of an opportunity to go home by accepting the bounty and re-enlisting. Some eighteen of Company D took advantage of the offer, among them E. M. Stone, John D. Hare, J. W. Mullins, A. L. Fry, J. W. Hight, John W. East, R. H. Bane, J. B. Young, Tom Young, W. H. Layton, Tom Davenport, John Palmer, and the writer. Tom Young, Davenport, Layton and Palmer never returned—deserted.

On our return to the army we were accompanied by Christian Minnich, who enlisted in the company, having two sons therein. The question of re-enlistment was soon settled by an act of Congress, which placed every man in the Confederate states between the ages of 18 and 35 in the army for three years, or until the close of the war, retaining all that were under 18 and over 45 for ninety days, continuing the organizations then existing, with the right to elect regimental and company officers.

March 1, or thereabouts, in 1862, the enemy began to push his lines closer up, and to make more frequent reconnaissances, and to extend his lines toward Aquia Creek on the Potomac, on the right flank of the Confederate army, causing our commander uneasiness, no doubt, as to the tenableness of our position, and hence on or about the 10th of the month orders were issued to cook rations, and be prepared to march. The movement began three days later, with the head of the column directed toward Warrenton and the Rappahannock River, which was crossed the second or third day. At Centerville we left burning immense quantities of provisions and army supplies, of which later we stood in dire need, the inadequacy of transportation being the excuse for the destruction.

At a point either in Culpeper or Rappahannock, near where we one night encamped, was a distillery, of which some of our men took possession, procuring Old Man Riley Albert to make a run of applejack, with which they tanked up, then filled their canteens, with no way to transport the residue. Harry Snidow and others from a nearby store procured jars, with which they trudged along until the jars were emptied. No one was drunk, but the boys were happy and jolly.

Gordonsville, in Orange County, near the junction of what was then the Central and Orange and Alexandria railroad, was reached, where we went into camp.

CHAPTER X

- **The Stay Near Gordonsville.**
- **The March to Richmond and Journey to Yorktown.**
- **In the Trenches.**
- **Skirmishing and Night Alarms.**
- **Reorganization.**
- **The Retreat from Yorktown.**
- **The Old Lady's Prayer.**
- **Battle of Williamsburg.**
- **The Killed and Wounded.**
- **Forces and Numbers Engaged and Losses.**
- **Retreat up the Peninsula.**
- **Battle of Seven Pines.**
- **Casualties.**

Our stay in the vicinity of Gordonsville was of short duration—only for a few days—for on or about April 1 we set out for Richmond, distant about seventy-five miles. The route taken lay through the counties of Louisa, Hanover and Henrico, a low, flat, swampy territory, and in March and April knee deep in mud. The people along this march were unaccustomed to seeing large bodies of armed men marching. The negroes, especially, gazed upon us with seeming astonishment. How long we were making this march to the capital city is not now recollected, but as we carried heavy burdens at that day, it is probable we did not reach Richmond before the 8th or 9th of April.

On the 10th of the month last mentioned, the 7th regiment left Richmond aboard a steamer on the James River, disembarking at King's Landing, ten miles from Yorktown, inland, whither we marched the evening of our debarkation. We took position in and near the trenches for the purpose of preventing the Federal army from marching up the peninsula. Now and then a brisk skirmish would occur on some part of the lines, scarcely a night passing without picket firing and alarms; one of which occurred during a heavy rainstorm, in which the men stood to their guns throughout the night and were thoroughly drenched by the rain.

The time for reorganization of the army had arrived, and this was accomplished quietly on Saturday, April 26, 1862, in the face of the enemy. Before giving in detail the result of the reorganization, I will state that a very decided change had taken place among the men as to their estimates of the character and ability of their officers, field and company. Many were moved by their dislikes and prejudices, engendered by contact in their first year's service, against officers who had endeavored to enforce obedience and strict military discipline, prompted by no other motive than the good of the service; yet these acts, done in accordance with military law, and inspired by patriotism, were often misconstrued by men born freemen, wholly unaccustomed to having restraints placed upon their personal liberty; such acts, the exercise of such authority, being regarded by our volunteer citizen soldiery as tyrannical. Consequently those who had been foremost in rushing to the country's rescue in the early days of her peril, bravely leading their men to the forefront of the battle, were displaced, to the detriment of the service; but patriotic and good men are oftentimes only human. The organization was, however, effected apparently without injury to the public service.

Captain James H. French, of my company, was taken sick on the march from the Rappahannock, and was left in Richmond; consequently he was not present at the reorganization, and perhaps was not a candidate for re-election. Had he been present and a candidate, it is more than probable he would have been again chosen captain without opposition, as no one could have had any personal grievance against him. He had proven himself a man of unflinching courage, and as much in this respect could be said of the other company officers. Save one, Lieutenant Joel Blackard, all were displaced. Blackard, in the reorganization, was elected captain; Sergeant R. H. Bane, first lieutenant; Orderly Sergeant John W. Mullins, second lieutenant; Corporal E. M. Stone, third lieutenant. The non-commissioned officers elected were: A. L. Fry, first sergeant; W. H. H. Snidow, second sergeant; William D. Peters, third sergeant; Joseph C. Shannon, fourth sergeant; this scribe, fifth sergeant; A. J. Thompson, first corporal; Daniel Bish, second corporal; George C. Mullins, third corporal, and J. B. Young, fourth corporal.

Comment as to the choice of the men will not here be made, nor the character of the new officers, as ample opportunity will be afforded in these pages to judge their conduct. It suffices to say now that the company had no cause for regret.

Of the regimental officers, Colonel James L. Kemper was chosen to succeed himself; Major W. T. Patton was elected lieutenant-colonel; Adjutant C. C. Flowerree, major; Lieutenant Starke was appointed adjutant; George S. Tansill, sergeant-major. Dr. C. B. Morton was regimental surgeon, with Dr. Oliver assistant, and upon the promotion of Dr. Morton to brigade surgeon, Dr. Oliver became regimental surgeon, with Dr. Worthington as assistant.

As recollected, Company H, from the District of Columbia, having served its one year, for which it had enlisted, disbanded shortly after reorganization.

Lieutenant-Colonel Lewis B. Williams, than whom no braver man wore the gray, was elected colonel of the 1st Virginia regiment. Prior to the battles of Bull Run and Manassas, the 7th regiment had been brigaded with the 24th Virginia and 7th Louisiana, under Colonel J. A. Early. After these battles, we were commanded by General Ewell. Subsequently, the 1st, 7th, 11th and 17th Virginia regiments formed General Longstreet's brigade. On reaching Yorktown, Brigadier-General A. P. Hill became our brigade commander, General Longstreet having been made a major-general, to whose division our brigade was attached.

At this juncture we were still at Yorktown, with the enemy bold and threatening in our front. It was evident, therefore, that a collision was imminent, either where we were or near by. The order came to move on Saturday evening, May 3. We were soon on the road, in the mud, floundering and pushing toward Williamsburg, about twelve miles distant, reaching there early next morning, after an all night march. The command halted in front of the grounds of the Eastern Hospital for the Insane. The enemy, evidently determined we should not get away without trouble, followed closely, skirmishing briskly with the rear guard, which was continued throughout the afternoon. Then came the monotonous standing in line of battle from early dawn till near midday—a thing that always tries the patience of a soldier. The booming of artillery, and the rattling of small arms could be distinctly heard. As we passed over the street leading to William and Mary College, an elderly lady appeared on her porch, with clasped hands and eyes lifted heavenward, uttering for us, in simple, pathetic tones, a prayer to God for the protection of our lives in the coming conflict.

Beyond the College the column filed to the right into an open field, piled baggage, and then in battle line moved forward into the timber, receiving as we entered therein a shower of balls at close range, wounding a number of men. This onslaught was answered by a charge from us, which broke up the lines of the enemy, consisting in part of New York regiments, and drove him for more than a half mile through the woods into a body of fallen timber, in which was encountered a fresh line of battle. Some doubt at first existed as to who these people were. This was settled by the unfurling of their flag. At close quarters, the fight was desperate for more than two hours, in which our ammunition was expended, when General A. P. Hill ordered a charge with fixed bayonets, upon which the enemy (New Jersey men) were driven from the field; for a hand-to-hand charge is something fearful to contemplate. Being relieved by other troops, Hill's brigade retired to the line from which it had moved in the charge, from whence we withdrew during the night, continuing the retreat; for it will be remembered that the task in hand for us was the holding in check of the enemy—a force vastly superior to our own. In this day's work I fired 36 charges, by which my shoulder was pounded so that it was for a time completely disabled. This battle was fought for a safe retreat for our trains and for the army, and accomplished this purpose. We had beaten the enemy in our center, and on the right wing, while a portion, two regiments, of General Early's brigade had been repulsed by General Hancock's Federal brigade.

The forces engaged were, as stated by General Longstreet: Federals, 12,000; Confederates, 9,000. The casualties: Federal, 2,288; Confederate, 1,565. This engagement was called the Battle of Williamsburg, and will be remembered by the survivors whose eyes may fall upon these lines.

In Hill's brigade the loss was 326, of which 67 were killed, 245 wounded, 14 missing. The 7th Virginia lost 13 killed, 64 wounded, aggregate 77. In Company D, of the 7th Virginia, the loss was one killed, 14 wounded, as follows: Killed, William H. Stafford; wounded, Lieutenant E. M. Stone, and the following men of the line: Allen M. Bane, Charles W. Peck, Andrew J. Thompson, John A. Hale, John W. East, Isaac Hare, George Knoll, Anderson Meadows, Demarcus Sarver, William I. Wilburn, Edward Z. Yager, John Meadows, and the writer—who knows what it is to have a hot buckshot in his hand. Baldwin L. Hoge had the belt of his cartridge box severed and cut from the belt; several of the men had holes shot through their clothing. Sergeant Tapley P. Mays, of Company D, the ensign of the regiment, who bore the flag aloft throughout the battle, had the staff severed three times and the flag pierced by twenty-three balls, Mays escaping unscathed. For his gallant conduct on this field, he received the thanks of the commandant of the regiment, and his conduct was made the subject matter of a complimentary letter to him from the Governor of the state, promising that he should receive a fine sword for his gallant conduct.

The mud was deep, the movement slow, and when morning dawned we were only a few miles from the battlefield, halting occasionally in battle line in order to hold the enemy in check until our long train of wagons and artillery could get away. It must not be supposed that because we were wearied, covered with mud and hungry, that we were dispirited and gloomy. Such mental conditions could not then well exist among such a jolly set of fellows, for we had in each company one or more who would have their amusement, in a joke, a laugh, or a song, especially Bolton and George

Knoll (the Dutchman), who were clownish and full of fun. In passing along the roads and through the towns and villages, if a citizen with a high silk hat appeared, these clowns would call out: "Mister, come out of that hat; I know you are in there, for I see your feet!" Another would likely call out: "Mister, my bees are swarming; lend me your hat to hive them in." They sometimes ran across a man with high top boots. Then it was: "Come out of them boots! I know you are in them, for I see your head above." Occasionally they were paid back in their own coin. An old preacher, white-haired, with long white flowing beard, one day rode into camp, when one of these wags called out: "Boys, here is old Father Abraham," whereupon the old preacher said: "Young men, you are mistaken. I am Saul, the son of Kish, searching for his father's asses, and I have found them." The preacher had won, and nobody enjoyed the joke better than the fellows who had been beaten at their own game.

The Chickahominy was crossed by our troops May 9, when we went into camp at Clark's farm, and later near Howard's Grove, on higher and dryer ground, with better water. Here inactivity and hot weather brought on much sickness. It was from this camp that A. L. Sumner of Company D took "French furlough"—went without leave, to see his family, was arrested, brought back, courtmartialed, and sentenced for a term to Castle Thunder, a Confederate prison in Richmond for Confederate delinquents. On his return he made up for his delinquency. A. L. Fry, orderly-sergeant, was summoned as a witness against Sumner at his trial, and was thereby absent at the battle of Frazier's farm.

For several days preceding the 30th day of May, 1862, the weather had been very sultry, and during the night of that day there broke over the camp a violent electric storm, accompanied by a heavy downpour of rain, which flooded the quarters and submerged everything on the ground within the tents, compelling the men to stand on their feet for hours. The vivid flashes of electricity, the fearful peals of thunder, reminded one of the progress of a mighty battle, and was a fitting precursor of the morrow's bloody day.

At daylight, Saturday, May 31, came the order to march. Although we knew the enemy was in close proximity to Richmond and extending his lines closer, with the intention of investing the city, yet we were at a loss to determine where we were going, as we had not received orders to be ready to move. Much difficulty was encountered in crossing the small branches, which had overflowed their banks, but we finally made our way into the Williamsburg road, learning on the way from parties coming from the front that a battle was imminent. Hurrying forward at quickstep, turning to the right from the Williamsburg road, we found ourselves in line of battle on the edge of a swamp in a wood, where we remained until about 1 P.M., hearing the boom of cannon, and indistinctly the rattle of musketry, apparently far to our left. Not long after the hour mentioned, we were hurried away to the left to Seven Pines, where we soon found ourselves face to face with the enemy, in part the Federal division of General Silas Casey, whose earthworks and camp we carried, including some of his artillery. The forces engaged, as given by General Longstreet in his "Manassas to Appomattox," were: Union troops, 18,500; Confederates, 14,600; Union losses, 5,031; Confederate, 4,798. This engagement was called by the Confederates the Battle of Seven Pines.

I have not been able to secure my brigade or regimental loss but my company loss was: A. D. Manning, killed; Sergeant E. R. Walker, Privates Travis Burton, John W. Hight and Joseph Lewy, wounded. Our ensign, Mays, acted with his usual gallantry.

The right wing of the Confederate army, under General Longstreet, had defeated the left wing of the Union army, captured its intrenchments, guns and camp, and driven it for quite a distance, but the Confederate left wing had not been so fortunate as the right. In this battle, after we had broken General Casey's lines, some Union sharpshooters took cover in the swamp in our front, one of whom at about seventy-five yards fired at me, the ball grazing my cap.

A short time previous to the Battle of Seven Pines, our brigadier-general, A. P. Hill, had been made major-general. Colonel Kemper had been promoted to brigadier-general and was in command of the brigade during the above-mentioned engagement. General Joseph E. Johnston, commanding the Confederate army in this battle, was badly wounded, and General Robert E. Lee was appointed to succeed him in the command.

We left the battleground, as now recalled, on June 2, returning to camp, a few days after which the 24th Virginia regiment, which had been with Early's, then with Garland's brigade, was united with ours—now composed of the 1st, 7th, 11th, 17th and 24th Virginia regiments.

CHAPTER XI

- **Preparations for Active Field Service.**

- **Dress Parade and Speeches of General Kemper and Colonel Patton.**

- **Battles Around Richmond.**

- **Gaines' Mill or Cold Harbor.**

- **Frazier's Farm and Malvern Hill.**

- **Testing a Man's Courage.**

- **Casualties.**

- **In Pursuit of the Enemy.**

- **In Camp Near the Chickahominy.**

- **Sickness and Death.**

- **Threatening Attitude of the Enemy in Northern Virginia.**

- **Concentration of the Confederate Army on the Rappahannock.**

- **Pope's Bravado.**

Lieutenant Hugh M. Patton Succeeds Stark as Adjutant, and Sergeant Parke Appointed Sergeant-Major, Succeeding George S. Tansill.

Following the Battle of Seven Pines, and the period preceding the opening of the battles around Richmond, at Mechanicsville on June 26, all were engaged in drilling and gathering in absentees. Muskets were put in order, cartridge boxes, bayonets and gun straps were issued. Inspection of arms and accouterments, and dress parades were frequent, and the word went from lip to lip that something was up, that all this preparation meant business, and that right early.

Rations were cooked and distributed on Wednesday, June 25, and everything put in shape to move on short notice. Being on parade on the evening of the day last referred to, General Kemper and Colonel Patton made soul-stirring speeches, telling us that the great battle of the revolution was now to be fought, and if we were successful the Confederacy would be a free country, and we would all go home together; if beaten, the war must be prolonged for years.

Leaving camp in the early morning of the 26th, we marched in the direction of Mechanicsville bridge, on the Chickahominy, halting a short distance from the bridge under cover of timber on the roadside, from which we could, late in the afternoon, hear the roar of the battle at Mechanicsville beyond the river, then being fought by the Confederate division of General A. P. Hill and the Federal corps of Porter. As the darkness came on the flash of their guns could be seen distinctly, the battle continuing until nearly 9 o'clock. At dawn the firing across the river was renewed, continuing for a time. The movement of our force was then made across the bridge, following the track of the retreating foe, whose course was marked by the destruction of commissary stores. Reaching the vicinity of Gaines' Mill at noon, a line of battle was formed behind and near the crest of a low range of hills, hiding us from the view of the enemy. In our immediate front were the brigades of Pickett, Wilcox and Pryor, who were to lead the assault on our part of the line, with our brigade in support. Near the middle of the afternoon the battle opened with fury, raging with varying fortune until nearly dark, when our troops broke over the Union lines, forcing their men from the field: a victory dearly bought. Kemper's brigade was not called into action, though lying under fearful shelling, but fortunately we were just near enough the crest of the ridge to avoid the shells, which passed in most part over us. We suffered but little if any loss.

The Federals engaged in this battle numbered about 35,000; their loss in killed, wounded and missing, 7,000, besides twenty-two pieces of artillery which fell into our hands. The Confederates no doubt had the larger number engaged, and their casualties were, therefore, greater, but seem not to have been reported.

Next morning we marched over the field on which the Confederate brigades of Wilcox, Pickett and Pryor, with others, had made heroic fight, and it is almost incredible that a single line of Confederates should have forced their way in the face of the murderous fire they met, over such a position, which was to all appearances impregnable, and certainly was, except as against men fighting for homes, firesides, and principles which they regarded as dearer than life.

We occupied the field Saturday, in a position to make or to receive an attack, but the enemy was in no plight—in fact, in no mood, to attack us, but on the contrary was making for the James River, though we did not then know it. Our officers did not seem to know with certainty what direction the enemy was taking, as his movement was well masked. It seems to have been discovered late on the evening of Saturday, the 28th, or early on Sunday morning, the 29th, that General McClellan, with his army, was making for the shelter of the Union naval fleet on the James, and such being the understanding, Longstreet's and A. P. Hill's divisions at an early hour on Sunday morning were pushed across the Chickahominy via New Bridge, and to the Darbytown road, to intercept the retreat. The day was warm, the roads dusty, and the march fatiguing, especially as it was rapid for fifteen or eighteen miles. Pushing ahead early the next day, Monday, June 30, the enemy was encountered about noon. The skirmishers were soon engaged, but the advance of our troops did not begin until about 4 o'clock P.M., and after we had suffered for two or more hours from a severe shelling. While under this severe fire and in line in the woods, in a swamp amidst brambles and vines, a shell from one of the enemy's guns burst immediately in our front and only a few feet away, scattering the fragments and shrapnel in our midst, one of which struck a man close by me, burying itself in a testament in his breast pocket, which thus saved his life.

Lieut. Elisha M. Stone

The point where the encounter took place was known locally as Frazier's farm. The only Confederate troops engaged were the two divisions above mentioned, which had been sorely reduced by the casualties at Seven Pines, Mechanicsville and Gaines' Mill, as well as by sickness, the exhaustion of a rapid march, and by straggling, to about 12,000 men. These were pitted against the main body of the Union army.

From the firing we had every reason to believe that the enemy was close at hand in large numbers, seemingly not distant more than half a mile. The advance of our forces was through a dense wood, tangled underbrush filled with brambles, and partly covered by water, with no possibility of keeping the men up to their places, the stronger ones pushing through over the obstacles, while many of the weaker, unable to keep pace, were left behind. Kemper's brigade was leading and his advance soon became a charge, the enemy being posted on the farther side of an open field. Some of the line officers implored the regimental commander to halt long enough to get the men in order and close the ranks, but the officer cried out: "Forward!

Forward!" and on rushed the men, every man his own general, which they usually were in making such a charge.

In a fierce battle a man's courage is severely tested. Here our regiment is in battle line on the edge of a wood; less than a quarter of a mile in front is another wood, sheltering the enemy; between the opposing forces is an open field; the regiment is advancing and the lines move out into the clear sunlight. Men will hurriedly reason with themselves: "The enemy is posted in that timber across the field; before we move many yards he will open on us with shot and shell; this is perhaps my last day on earth." So each man reasons, but every face is sternly set to the front and not a man falters. The shell and shot blow dozens to gory fragments, but the line does not halt, the living saying to themselves: "The fire will presently change to cannister, then I shall certainly be struck." The prediction is being verified, gaps are opened through the ranks, only to be closed again; the regiment has lost its adhesion and marching step, its lines are no longer perfect, but the movement is still onward. From knowledge of methods in battle, our men suppose the infantry is in support of the battery. We have escaped shell and cannister, but when we meet the musketry fire we shall be killed. There is no hanging back, no thought but to push ahead. The leaden hail now comes and the lines are further disordered; the left wing has lost its front by quite a distance, but the push is forward, men grip their guns, their eyes flash, and with a yell, on to the battery they rush, bayonetting the cannoneers at their posts. The Federal infantry supports give way precipitately—then follows that famous bone-searching rebel yell of triumph.

The brigade, led by the brave General Kemper, met a shower of shot, shell, cannister and storm of leaden bullets; it never faltered, rushed upon the Union battery—Randol's Pennsylvania—routing its infantry supports. Here Ensign Mays planted the colors of the 7th regiment on the Union guns. They were ours, won, however, at fearful cost. The failure promptly to support our brigade—the enemy flanking us on both wings—caused General Kemper to order the retirement of the brigade, now suffering severe loss from the fire of these flanking columns, which in turn were themselves flanked and defeated by the troops coming to our support. Such is the fearful game of war with men of the same valor and blood.

The brigade casualties were 414, of which 44 were killed, 205 wounded and 165 missing. Regimental loss in the 7th Virginia, 111, of which 14 were killed, 66 wounded and 31 missing. Adjutant E. B. Starke was killed and Sergeant-Major Tansill severely wounded, disabled for further service. Sergeant-Major Tansill had been a soldier in our war with Mexico, and was one of the most efficient, the bravest and best of our soldiers. The gallant

Lieutenant, afterwards Captain James G. Tansill, of Company E, of the 7th regiment, was the son of Sergeant-Major Tansill.

The loss in my company was 16. Killed, Captain Joel Blackard; mortally wounded, Ballard P. Meadows, Lee E. Vass and Joseph Eggleston; the other wounded were: J. C. Shannon, Daniel Bish, Jesse B. Young, David C. Akers, H. J. Wilburn, Tim P. Darr, Francis M. Gordon, George A. Minnich, T. P. Mays, John W. Sarver and Joseph Suthern. Captured, Allen M. Bane. Ballard P. Meadows was made a prisoner and died in the hands of the enemy. Upon the fall of the brave and lamented Captain Blackard, the command of the company devolved upon First Lieutenant Robert H. Bane, a gallant soldier, and a worthy successor to Captain Blackard. Second Lieutenant Mullins became first lieutenant; E. M. Stone, second lieutenant, and Sergeant E. R. Walker was elected second junior lieutenant.

During that night our troops rested on the field without disturbance from the enemy, who continued his flank movement, a masterly retreat, to a position at Malvern Hill, on the banks of the James: a position of great natural strength, where the entire Union army was concentrated, supported by the gunboats in the river. The Battle of Malvern Hill did not begin until the afternoon, but its tide swept to and fro until far into the night. The divisions of Longstreet and A. P. Hill were held in reserve, close up, but not called into action, near enough, however, to be in range of the enemy's artillery and heavy projectiles thrown from the gunboats, inspiring fear and terror among our men not justified by their execution. The repeated charges of our troops against the enemy's stronghold failed to dislodge him. Our men were repulsed; they had bearded the lion in his den; he refused to yield; he could not afford to, for if he did he had but one place to go and that was into the river, or the alternative, of surrendering. In the Battle of Frazier's Farm the Federals largely outnumbered the Confederates. They lost ten guns captured by the Confederates, who, when the battle closed, held the greater part of the field. The Federal General McCall was captured by the 47th Virginia regiment.

At the opening of the campaign, the Union army numbered 105,000, the Confederate 80,762—tremendous armies, when we come to think of it. The losses on each side, up to the Battle of Malvern Hill, in killed and wounded, were thought to be equal, but in that battle it is stated upon authority that the Confederate loss was about 5,000 men, the Union loss about one-third that number. During the Battle of Malvern Hill, Mr. Davis, President of the Confederate States, was with us in the morning and under the fire of the gunboats.

It being ascertained that the enemy had retreated during the previous night, we hastened in pursuit, amidst a heavy rainstorm, and after a fatiguing, disagreeable, all-day march, found the enemy in a strong position at Westover, on the James. As he showed no disposition to come out from his cover, our army, about July 8, reached its camps in the vicinity of Richmond. It had been a wonderful series of battles. General McClellan had made a most masterly retreat, escaping from woeful disaster. It was within the range of probability, in fact, almost a certainty, that if the Confederate army had been under as good discipline as it was two years later, the Union army would have been destroyed or made prisoners. As it was, the Federal loss was nearly 16,000 men and 54 pieces of artillery, while the Confederate loss was reckoned at about 19,000 men. Richmond had been saved, the enemy driven far away, General McClellan proving himself better at a retreat than going the other way.

After the enemy had taken shelter under the protection of his gunboats at Westover, the Confederate commissariat attempted to reach the large amount of supplies held by the farmers along the James River. Numerous wagons were sent under escort to secure these supplies. Our Company D, going on one of these trips, was attacked by Union gunboats, into which we fired quite a number of volleys of musketry at close range, being sheltered by the river bank, and in return received a severe shelling. A few men were wounded, and I received a shot on the side of the foot, but not much of a hurt.

From July 8 to August 13, a period of inactivity ensued, and as usual in that swampy country, with bad water, there was much sickness among the men. Lewis R. Skeens, of Company D, died in camp and was buried near by. Charles W. Peck, George W. Akers, William C. Fortner, James B. Henderson, John R. Crawford, and the writer were taken sick and sent to hospital at Richmond, where Peck and Akers died. Fortner, Henderson, Crawford and the writer improved rapidly, and were ready to return to our command by the middle of August.

General McClellan's Union army was shut up at Westover, and being depleted by the ravages of sickness and death. This fact, together with the threatening attitude of a new Federal army in Northern Virginia, induced General Lee, who now had apparently nothing to fear from McClellan, to concentrate his army on the Rappahannock, and to that end about the middle of July had transferred General Jackson and his command to the Rapidan—which, by the early days of August, was in the vicinity of the enemy—and closed with him at Cedar Mountain on August 9, forcing the enemy to retire on Culpeper court house.

Longstreet's division left Richmond Wednesday, August 13, for Gordonsville and the Rapidan, our brigade moving by rail. Learning that our division was moving, Fortner, Henderson, Crawford and the writer, the sick bunch above alluded to, applied for discharge from the hospital, and procured transportation via Lynchburg. Reaching Orange court house on the 18th, we left the railway, taking the track of the advancing army. The first day's tramp finished up Fortner and Henderson, both of whom were still feeble; and it also finished up my shoes, leaving me barefoot; in fact, had none I could wear until after our return from Maryland a month later. Leaving Fortner and Henderson on the road, Crawford and I pushed on, rejoining our command on the Rappahannock. Fortner overtook us in a few days, and in time to go into the battle of the 30th, when he received a severe wound. Poor Fortner! Misfortune seemed now to be his lot, going and coming.

By August 20 the greater part of General Lee's army was on the Rappahannock, confronting the Union army under General John Pope, on the opposite bank. Pope, who, it is stated, had said a few days before in an address to his troops that "his headquarters were in the saddle, and that he never turned his back upon an enemy nor looked for lines of retreat"—which statement he later denied—had already run, and was in a position to have to run again, or at least to get to the rear to look after his line of retreat.

Longstreet's division on August 21 moved forward to Kelley's ford, which we left on the 22d, taking position near Beverly's, relieving some of General Jackson's command, which moved up the Rappahannock. For three or four days there was considerable skirmishing, with occasional artillery duels across the river. Again moving on the 24th to the assistance of Jackson's troops, engaged with the enemy at some of the upper fords of the Rappahannock, our march was retarded by the swollen condition of Hazel river and other small tributaries of the Rappahannock; reaching Jeffersonton that afternoon, during the progress of a lively cannonade. A halt was made by our division and Jackson's men moved up the river. Lieut. Hugh M. Patton had been appointed Adjutant of the seventh regiment, succeeding Adjutant Starke, and —— Park had been appointed Sergeant Major to succeed George S. Tansill, disabled and discharged.

CHAPTER XII

- General Jackson With His "Foot Cavalry."

- On the Flank and in the Rear of General Pope's Army.

- Longstreet's Division Diverting the Enemy's Attention on the Rappahannock.

- March Through Thoroughfare Gap.

- Haymarket to the Relief of Jackson's Men.

- The Fight on the 29th.

- Battle of August 30, 1862.

- Kemper Commands Division, Corse Leads the Brigade.

- Pope Defeated.

- Casualties.

- Rainstorm and March Through Leesburg to White's Ford.

- Crossing the Potomac.

- The Cry "Back to Washington" and not "On to Richmond."

- "Maryland, My Maryland," "Bonnie Blue Flag."

- Halt at Monocacy Bridge.

General Jackson with his "foot cavalry," as his men were often referred to, on account of their rapid marches and power of endurance, crossed the Rappahannock on August 25 and by swift marches placed his command at Manassas in the rear of General Pope's army, and between it and Washington—our division (Longstreet's) amusing General Pope on the Rappahannock by making sortie in order to divert his attention from General Jackson's movement.

Longstreet's division crossed the river near Amissville on Tuesday, the 26th, reaching Thoroughfare Gap in the afternoon of the 28th; the march having been somewhat disturbed by a body of the enemy's cavalry. The enemy held the east side of the Gap in large force. The evening was spent in reconnoitering, getting into position to carry the Gap. Our rations consisted of green corn and fresh beef. Numbers of the men were without shoes, including the writer. Some horses belonging to the wagons or ambulances broke from their fastenings during the night, running through the camp and creating quite a stir, as someone called out, "Yankee Cavalry!" No damage was done, except the loss of an ear by one man from the stroke of a horse's hoof. The man yelled, "I've got a one *ear* furlough."

The Gap next morning was flanked by our troops, the enemy scurrying away in time to save his face. After clearing the Gap and reaching the vicinity of the little village of Haymarket, there could be heard distinctly seven or eight miles away the roar of artillery. The day was warm, the roads dusty, and the men suffered for water. It was pathetic to see the boys with feet bare and bleeding endeavoring to keep pace with their comrades.

A little past noon on the 29th, we arrived in the vicinity of the battleground, and not long thereafter the roar of battle to our left informed us that Jackson's men were hotly engaged. Later in the evening, the brigades of Hood and Evans, of Longstreet's division, engaged a portion of the enemy, driving him for some distance. The remainder of our division was in line of battle, prepared to attack, as we understood, a force of the enemy to the right, should opportunity offer. Our position was now between the Warrenton pike and Manassas Gap railway—where we were still subsisting on roasting ears and fresh beef; no large quantity at that, but the Confederate soldier ever bore his privations with less complaint than would be supposed by those who did not know his enthusiasm for cause and country.

On the morning of the 30th, during skirmishing and artillery fire along the lines, the command to which we belonged moved forward a short distance, resting near an old rail fence which ran on and along a narrow country road. All firing ceased about noon, and quiet continued until about 3 o'clock P.M., when it was broken by the lumbering of artillery and the crash of small arms. While lying on the road referred to, A. J. Thompson and John Q. Martin, of Company D, came near having a serious fight, which was finally terminated by the interference of Colonel Patton. In a few minutes after this trouble, the battle opened on the left, rolling towards us. The order came, and the brigade, under command of Colonel Corse, went forward at double quick, over a field, through the woods, and into open ground, where the enemy was in line of battle. The charge of the division under General Kemper, the brigade under Colonel Corse, was impetuous and most gallant, routing the Union infantry and capturing a Maine battery and some regimental flags. General Pope's army was defeated and in retreat. It was now dark. The forces engaged on the Union side, under General Pope, in this series of battles around Manassas amounted to 74,578 men; those on the side of the Confederates, 49,077. The casualties in the Union army were 1,747 killed, 8452 wounded, 4263 missing; aggregate, 14,462. On the side of the Confederates, 1468 were killed, 7563 wounded, and 81 missing; aggregate, 9112. Thirty Union field guns were captured by the Confederates, with 20,000 small arms, including a number of colors.

Our brigade loss was 33 killed, 240 wounded, and one missing; aggregate, 274. The regimental loss was Col. W. T. Patton, Lieut. Col. C. C. Flowerree, Major Swinler, Adjutant Patton and Sergt. Major Park, all of whom were severely wounded, Major Swinler losing a leg, and Adjutant Patton and Sergt. Major Park being disabled for further service. The loss including those mentioned was five killed, 48 wounded; aggregate 53.

The loss in my company was 16, equal to about one-third of the regimental loss: John Q. Martin, killed; wounded, Lieutenant John W. Mullins and 14 privates, viz: William H. Carr, John S. Dudley, Elbert S. Eaton, Adam Thompson, William C. Fortner, James H. Fortner, Francis H. Farley, J. Tyler Frazier, John W. Hight, G. L. Wilburn, H. J. Wilburn, William I. Wilburn, James J. Nye and Washington R. C. Vass. The two latter were mortally wounded, Vass dying that night and Nye a few days thereafter. A. L. Fry had been sent with our wounded Lieutenant Mullins to Warrenton, and was there captured by the enemy after the army had crossed the Potomac.

I must speak here of some little incidents in connection with this battle which I think worthy of notice. The advance of the brigade in the charge encountered a rail fence, a short distance beyond which was the enemy's battery, and its battle line of infantry supports. When near the fence, fearless Lieutenant-Colonel Flowerree—a mere boy, scarcely 21 years of age—shouted: "Up to the fence, 7th regiment, and give them h—l!"

In closing on the battery, the man at the breach was in the act of firing, when bold Ike Hare, of my company, directly in front of the guns, cried out, "Fire!" Whiz! went the ball over the heads of the men, who the next moment, with Colonel Skinner of the First Virginia regiment, were among the cannoneers, the Colonel, with heavy sabre in hand, cutting right and left, receiving a wound in the encounter which retired him from the service.

I went out to help gather up the wounded, and to get me a pair of trousers and shoes, both of which I had need of, and which I procured, selecting a dead Union soldier about my size. His shoes I could not wear, as they were too small, and I gave them to a comrade; and I almost regretted having put on his trousers, for they were inhabited by the same sort of graybacks common to the Confederate and Union soldiers. After more than 50 years the thought of this wretched parasite makes my flesh itch. But these pests were unavoidable to soldiers continually on the march through mud, mire, and over dusty roads, without opportunity to cleanse their clothes or make a change thereof, and this was particularly so with the Confederate soldier, who seldom had, or could procure a change of raiment.

In front of our regiment fell mortally wounded Colonel Fletcher Webster, of Massachusetts, the only son of Daniel Webster, where he lay until next day.

As was usual following the great battles of our war, there came down that night, and continuing the most of the next two days, a heavy downpour of rain; a great blessing to the wounded, who needed the cooler temperature, as some relief at least from the warm and oppressive heat.

Our time on Sunday was occupied in burying the dead and caring for the wounded, then being relieved by others. On Monday, September 1, followed the command of General Jackson to Chantilly, where he had a heavy engagement with the enemy. From here we marched on the 3d, 4th and 5th, passing through Leesburg and to White's Ford on the Potomac River, where camp was made on the evening of the 5th.

At Leesburg an order came for all sick and shoeless men to remain there: an unfortunate order, in some respects, as it was construed by a great many of the men to mean just anyone who did not want to go over the river into Maryland. There had already been large depletion of the ranks, after leaving Richmond, caused by straggling—partly by shoeless and sick men, and partly, doubtless, from other causes. Rapid marching and insufficient, indifferent, or no food, had much to do with the straggling. Judging other commands by my own, I can state that much too large a number of men remained at Leesburg, stretching the pretext to cover far more than was intended by the order. But when it is remembered that the army within a period of ninety days had fought not less than eleven pitched battles, sustaining losses in the aggregate of fully thirty-five thousand men, and that in addition to this they had engaged in many skirmishes, in which numbers of men were lost, and that the use of bad water and bad or insufficient food had depleted the ranks by thousands; and again, further considering that a large portion of the army had marched from Richmond to the Potomac, hundreds shoeless and more becoming so—it is not strange there were so many stragglers, sick and barefooted men. They amounted to probably 20,000. I think a great many remained at Leesburg who were not sick or barefoot, because of their aversion to fighting beyond Virginia territory, north of the Potomac. In one or more of these things enumerated, I may say thousands of men found excuses, or made them, to fall out of ranks along the line of march, finally to halt at Leesburg—men whose help was sorely needed at Sharpsburg.

The Potomac River was forded on the morning of September 6, amid the singing of "Maryland, My Maryland," and the shouts and cheering of the men. "Back to Washington," the cry, instead of "On to Richmond," which we had heard from our foes. Winchester was made the rendezvous for all the sick, lame, shoeless and others who remained as we passed Leesburg.

That night we camped at a little village, or crossroad hamlet, I think called Buckeystown. Next day, the 7th, a halt was made at the railway bridge over the Monocacy, two miles or more from Frederick, Maryland. Many of the shoeless, and others too plucky to remain at Leesburg, still kept their places with their comrades, following the fortunes of the army throughout the campaign. I was one of the number that made this tramp with bare feet.

CHAPTER XIII

A Musket, cartridge box with forty rounds of cartridges, cloth haversack, blanket and canteen made up the Confederate soldier's equipment. No man was allowed a change of clothing, nor could he have carried it. A gray cap, jacket, trousers and colored shirt—calico mostly—made up a private's wardrobe. When a clean shirt became necessary, we took off the soiled one, went to the water, usually without soap, gave it a little rubbing, and if the sun was shining, hung the shirt on a bush to dry, while the wearer sought the shade to give the shirt a chance. The method of carrying our few assets was to roll them in a blanket, tying each end of the roll, which was then swung over the shoulder. At night this blanket was unrolled and wrapped around its owner, who found a place on the ground with his cartridge box for a pillow. We cooked but little, having usually little to cook. The frying pan was in use, if we had one.

We remained three days at Monocacy, during which time the bridge was destroyed by our engineers. The morning of Wednesday, September 10, our division marched through Frederick, Middletown, Boonsboro, and to Hagerstown, reaching the latter place the evening of the 11th, and going into camp half a mile to the south of the town. Subsistence was still a pressing need, green corn and fresh beef becoming monotonous.

In Frederick our hearts were made glad by unmistakable signs of friendship and sympathy. A bevy of pretty girls, singing "Maryland, My Maryland," on seeing our battle flag inscribed "Seven Pines," proposed "three cheers for the battle flag of Seven Pines," which were heartily and lustily given by us. In Middletown we met no smiles, but a decided Union sentiment was in evidence. In Hagerstown we observed indications and heard some expressions of Southern sentiment, but none that satisfied us that they were ready and willing to shed their blood for the Southern cause.

The troops of Stonewall Jackson, together with those of McLaws and Walker, were now rapidly moving to invest and capture the Union garrison of some 13,000 men, at Harper's Ferry. During the march from Frederick, the Confederate rear was protected by a cavalry force under General Stuart, and infantry under General D. H. Hill. In the wake of this rear guard, following leisurely was the Union army under General McClellan, quite a hundred thousand strong, including a powerful artillery of 300 guns.

On Sunday, just before noon of the 14th, the long roll sounded calling the men into line, and a quick movement was made east in the direction of Boonsboro and Turner's Gap. Wagons, artillery and ambulances cleared the road, giving us the right of way. At Hagerstown was left General Toombs' Georgia brigade, and one regiment of G. T. Anderson's to watch a Federal gathering force just across the Maryland line. The day was hot, the road hard and dusty, the march rapid—so much so that many of the men broke down, falling by the wayside. The emergency demanded the presence of our division on the field of battle, which we knew, having learned on our way that General Hill's division had been attacked at Turner's Gap beyond Boonsboro by a largely superior force, perhaps by the larger part of General McClellan's Union army. Let it now be remembered that this army made fourteen miles to the immediate vicinity of the battleground in three and a half hours—good time for a Hamiltonian horse. Now with other troops we were hurried up the mountain to the right of the main gap (Turner's), and after getting near the firing line, and finding Confederate troops there holding the enemy in steady fight, our steps were retraced to the Gap. From thence we were ordered to the left, climbing the mountain side in full view of the enemy to our right, and in range of one of his batteries on a plateau to our right rear, which threw shot and shell thick and fast, striking the head of the leading company of my regiment and killing one man instantly. On reaching the crest of the mountain we found ourselves face to face with the enemy and close up to them, and under fire before we were able to get into formation. The brigades of Rodes and Evans on the left were engaged in strong combat with the force in their front, and as soon as Garnett's and Jenkins' brigades filled the space on the right and connected with Colquit's Georgia brigade, which was astride the turnpike, the fighting along the line became general and fierce, as much so as brave men on both sides could make it.

The writer's brigade was now in a body of open timber, among stones— large boulders, with some fallen timber along the line, behind which, lying down, the men took shelter as best they could; the enemy occupying a skirt of woods with a strip of open land between their position and ours. For two or more hours the battle raged, or until darkness fell, the enemy making repeated but unsuccessful efforts to dislodge our men. The firing having ceased, there was heard in our front the tramp of the enemy's feet, evidently preparing to renew the assault. In a few minutes, a few yards to the right, in which lay a portion of the brigade in the edge of a field, where at the beginning of the battle was standing corn (now cut to the ground) came the sound of a voice, "There they are, men! Fire on them!" Suddenly came a sheet of flame with a deafening crash from the guns of each of the combatants, plainly disclosing them to be within a few feet of each other. The flame from the respective muskets seemed to intermingle. The well-directed fire of the Confederates caused confusion in the enemy's ranks and compelled them to retire. Among the casualties on our side from this encounter was Adjutant John W. Daniel of the 11th Virginia, who received a severe wound in the hand. This same Daniel served with distinction in the United States Senate, dying a year or so ago. Such was the character of many a noble man engaged in this horrid game of death.

It was now 9 o'clock or after and intensely dark, especially in the timber where we were. Wounded comrades had to be removed and cared for; this had to be done quietly, as the enemy was in whispering distance. As heretofore stated, Company D of the 7th Virginia carried into the battle of Second Manassas forty men, of which sixteen were killed and wounded, leaving twenty-four, including commissioned officers. After crossing the Potomac and on entering the battle at Boonsboro Gap, we had twenty-one commissioned officers and men. In this battle were lost four men: T. P. Mays, killed; James Cole, mortally wounded; George Knoll, severely, and John R. Crawford, slightly wounded. Mays was serving in the capacity of ensign of the regiment, and died at the front, where danger was met and glory won, with that flag which he had so gallantly, proudly and defiantly borne aloft on many victorious fields. Brave and undaunted, he ever led where duty called, sharing the hardships and privations of camp life, the march and dangers of battle, without a murmur, and dying with his flag unfurled and its staff clenched in his hands. May the memory of Tapley P. Mays rest in peace.

With two commissioned officers, Captain Bane and Lieutenant Stone, and fifteen men we left the field a little after 9 o'clock at night, carrying one of the wounded, George Knoll, who had an ankle bone fractured. Knoll was borne on the back of Isaac Hare a mile or more to the hospital in Boonsboro.

The officers and men of Company D who went into the battle of Boonsboro were Capt. R. H. Bane, Lieut. E. M. Stone; men of the line, Travis Burton, John R. Crawford, James Cole, John S. Dudley, John A. Hale, Isaac Hare, B. L. Hoge, J. J. Hurt, John F. Jones, David E. Johnston, George Knoll, John Meadows, T. P. Mays, W. W. Munsey, William D. Peters, W. H. H. Snidow, R. M. Stafford, Thomas S. Taylor and A. J. Thompson. The cook in Company D, Alexander Bolton, remained with the supply trains and was not in the engagement.

The forces in this battle on the Federal side, according to the report of General McClellan, numbered 30,000, while the Confederate force, as stated by General D. H. Hill and others, was 9000. The Federal loss was 1813 in fifty-nine infantry regiments engaged; 325 killed, 1403 wounded, and 85 missing. The Confederate loss was 224 killed, 860 wounded, and 800 made prisoners. There are but few regimental reports of losses, therefore I am unable to give those in the 7th Virginia. I am satisfied that of the four brigades of Evans, Kemper, Garnett and Jenkins, sent late in the evening to reinforce the Confederate left, not more than one thousand men reached the firing line, but these were iron soldiers equal to the emergency, holding more than 5000 of the enemy at bay until we were ready to leave the field. The superb fighting in this battle—if at this day a fight can be called something superb—prevented the enemy from occupying the Gap, thus sealing the fate of the Union garrison at Harper's Ferry, which surrendered the following morning, the tidings whereof came to us about noon, causing much rejoicing.

Now set in an all night's march to the scene of the struggle at Sharpsburg, called in the North "Antietam," among the most gigantic and awful in the history of warfare. When daylight came Monday, we were at Keedysville, midway between the points mentioned, not having reached the field of Sharpsburg until 12 o'clock. Having been on our feet all night, without sleep or food, save green corn or apples, placed us in no cheerful mood, but in good fighting temper, as hungry soldiers fight better than well fed ones. Numbers of men straggled off along the march, and even after the Antietam was crossed, in search of food, a number of whom did not get back in the ranks for the battle.

Lieut. John W. Mullins

CHAPTER XIV

- **Number of Men for Action in Kemper's Brigade.**

- **General D. R. Jones' Division.**

- **Confederate Cavalry.**

- **General Lee Playing Bluff with McClellan.**

- **The Opening of the Battle.**

- **Burnside's Attack and Repulse.**

- **The Casualties.**

- **Re-crossing the Potomac.**

When Kemper's brigade was called to action at Sharpsburg, it did not number 400 muskets. The only regimental report accessible of the number going into action and the loss is that of Colonel Corse of the 17th Virginia (himself wounded), who says he led into the action fifty-five officers and men, all of whom were lost but five. The 1st Virginia did not number more than 30, the 11th Virginia 85, the 24th probably 110, and I know (for I counted them) that the 7th Virginia had but 117, Company D having but two commissioned officers and fifteen men before action began. Sergeant Taylor, sent in quest of rations, did not return with the food until the battle had ended. John S. Dudley, on the skirmish line, was wounded and captured. He, with Taylor, made the fifteen, leaving for battle two officers and thirteen men. Kemper's brigade belonged to General D. R. Jones' division, which was composed of the brigades of Jenkins, Garnett, Jones, under Colonel Geo. T. Anderson, Drayton, Kemper and Toombs, numbering on that morning, by the report of General Jones, 2400 men— far too many.

The division of General Jones held the ground in front and southeast of Sharpsburg, extending from the Boonsboro-Sharpsburg pike along the ridges and range of hills in front, south and east of the old road to Harper's Ferry, nearly a mile in length, covering the approaches from what has since been known as Burnside's bridge over the Antietam. Robertson's cavalry brigade, under Colonel Thomas T. Munford, was in observation on the extreme right along the Antietam and toward the Potomac; General Stuart, with General Fitzhugh Lee's cavalry brigade, the 13th Virginia regiment of infantry, with a number of batteries holding the extreme Confederate left, Hampton's cavalry brigade not in the fight, but in reserve, in rear of Stuart's position.

It is stated upon authority that during Monday, September 15, and for most of Tuesday, the 16th, General Lee confronted General McClellan's Union army with only the divisions of Longstreet and D. H. Hill, numbering all told 10,000 men, while General McClellan had 60,000 men then facing Lee.

In the afternoon of Monday, and continuing for the most of Tuesday, the Federal batteries across the Antietam kept up a lively fire, during which the troops, our brigade included, frequently shifted position, showing our flags first at one and then at another place, being exposed to the artillery fire, and getting a severe shelling. General Lee was playing bluff with McClellan, who was led to believe—and so reported to his government—that he was confronted not only by "a strong position, but by a strong force"—imaginary numbers, not real.

Late in the evening of Tuesday the firing to the left seemed to increase. We heard not only the artillery fire but the rattle of musketry for quite a time after dark. Before daylight on Wednesday, the 17th, the artillery opened vigorously on the left, followed by the crash of small arms, the battle raging with intense fury for hours. From our position on the right we could not see the combatants, but could hear the crash of small arms and the wild rebel yell. As long as we could hear this yell we felt that things were going our way.

The battle which began on the left had at noon extended to the right until the Confederate troops holding the open ground on the left front of Sharpsburg were within our view. We discovered at this time a straggling retreating line of Confederates closely followed by a solid blue line, which soon met the fire of a Confederate battery, causing it to retire.

Now affairs in our front began to claim our attention. The 24th Virginia regiment was detached from the brigade and sent a half mile to the right, and shortly thereafter the 7th Virginia under Captain Phil S. Ashby was detached and hurried to the right, taking position in front of the old road leading from Sharpsburg to Harper's Ferry, between the position held by the 1st, 11th and 17th Virginia regiments of the brigade, and that held by the 24th regiment. Upon the advance of the enemy we dropped back into the old road referred to. Captain Ashby had been a soldier in our war with Mexico, was a brave man, and when he had placed the regiment in the road, seeing the advance of the enemy he drew his sword, saying: "Men, we are to hold this position at all hazards. Not a man leave his place. If need be, we will die together here in this road." Putting our muskets through the board fence, and with fingers on the triggers, we awaited the enemy's approach through a strip of corn, some forty yards away.[4]

Colonel Geo. T. Anderson's brigade of D. R. Jones' division had early in the morning been detached and sent to the aid of General Jackson, and

Garnett's brigade had been taken away and placed in position to cover the front of Sharpsburg. General Lee had stripped his right in aid of his left, which was being sorely pressed, leaving General Jones to hold the right with the small brigades of Jenkins, Garnett, Drayton, Kemper and Toombs, whose numbers I will later attempt to give.

Two of General Toombs' regiments, the 15th and 17th Georgia, were guarding ammunition trains, and he, with the 2d and the 20th Georgia, and 50th Georgia of Drayton's brigade—in all numbering 403 men—with a company of sharpshooters and a battery, was ordered to the defense of the bridge (Burnside's). On Wednesday morning at an early hour General Burnside, who had been ordered to carry the bridge and advance to the heights at Sharpsburg, assailed General Toombs' men at the bridge. The stream is small, and at the time of the battle afforded but little water—could have been waded in dozens of places. Why the bridge? Burnside made the effort to carry the bridge, was five times repulsed by Toombs' small force, losing a large number of men in killed and wounded—exacting, however, from Toombs' regiments heavy toll, for his 2d Georgia lost one-half its numbers, and the 20th Georgia suffered heavily. General Toombs, finding the enemy crossing the stream at a ford below the bridge, and the position no longer tenable, withdrew his men and retired to the heights on which Jones' four brigades—Jenkins', Garnett's, Drayton's and Kemper's—were posted. General Toombs was joined on the way by his 15th and 17th Georgia, and Major Little's battalion of 140 Georgia men. His 20th Georgia had been sent to replenish its ammunition, and only part of these men returned in time for the final contest.

The enemy came in bold march at 4 P.M. He came in fine style and good order until probably half way from the Antietam to the crest of the heights, whereon stood the depleted Confederate battalions of Jenkins, Garnett, Drayton and Kemper, when he encountered the Confederate skirmish line posted behind stone and rail fences. These skirmishes repulsed and routed the Union skirmishers, making it so hot for the enemy's front battle line that it was only able to push forward by its mere momentum, but on it came, overrunning, killing, wounding and capturing the entire skirmish line, the men thereof remaining in their places, firing until he reached the muzzles of their muskets. The enemy's battle line overreached Kemper's right by several hundred yards, exposing McIntosh's battery, the men thereof for the time being forced to abandon their guns. Kemper's and Drayton's men were broken off, outflanked and forced back to the outskirts of the village.

General A. P. Hill with five small Confederate brigades which had left Harper's Ferry that morning, marching seventeen miles, reached the field at the opportune moment. Leaving two of his brigades to guard the approach from a ford on his right, General Hill threw the brigades of Gregg, Archer and Branch on the enemy's left front and flank, while General Toombs, who had circled around the enemy's left, being joined by the men of Kemper, Jenkins, Garnett and Drayton, together with Hill's three brigades, with a wild yell charged, the Confederate batteries opening fiercely; the enemy was driven from the field, mostly in disorder, fleeing to the banks of the Antietam for shelter. The field was won, the day was ours. In this headlong Confederate charge, General Branch of Hill's division was killed; General Gregg of the same division and General Toombs of Jones' division, wounded. Federal General Rodman was mortally wounded. The 24th and 7th Virginia suffered a few casualties in killed and wounded, mostly from the artillery fire, a few by musket balls. My company lost Hare, and Dudley wounded, the latter captured on the skirmish line.

With the utter defeat of General Burnside's Federal Army Corps, the battle ended, and Kemper's brigade occupied that night and the next day the same position it held when the battle in our front opened.

No fiercer, bloodier one day's conflict occurred during the war than the battle of Sharpsburg, which was fought on the part of the Confederates by a worn out, broken down, naked, barefooted, lame and starved soldiery, against a far superior force of brave, well rested, well clothed and well fed veterans. It was an all day, stand up, toe-to-toe and face-to-face fight, just as close as brave American soldiers could make it, and in none other did Southern individuality and self reliance—characteristics of the Confederate soldier—shine more brilliantly or perform a more important part. It was on this field that strategy and military science won the day for the Confederates. It was mind over matter. General Lee, the greatest military man of the age, was on the field, wielding the blade that was so admirably tempered, which brought blood and destruction at every stroke.

The failure of the Union soldiers to win this battle and utterly crush the Confederates, was no fault of theirs; they had the numbers and equipment, were courageous and brave. The truth is, their leader was timid, overcautious, and outgeneraled, fought his battle in detail, and was defeated in detail. General Burnside's, the largest single attacking corps, was beaten before he had his columns fairly deployed, and this because the Confederates outmaneuvered him on the field, had the flanks of his assaulting columns turned before he knew there was any Confederate force on the ground to turn them. Upon this occurring, he lost control of the battle, and the only thing apparent to him was to get away as quickly as possible, which he did, though his battle had not lasted an hour.

The force engaged in this battle on the Confederate right, on the Union side, was that of General Burnside's 9th army corps, consisting of twenty-nine regiments of infantry, six batteries of artillery, and two companies of cavalry, making, according to the most reliable information obtainable, an aggregate of 13,083. His losses were: Killed, 436; wounded, 1796; missing, 115; total, 2349.

On the Confederate side the battle was fought by the brigades of Jenkins, Garnett, Toombs, Kemper and Drayton (two regiments, 51st Georgia and 15th South Carolina); Gregg's, Archer's and Branch's (less the 18th North Carolina, on detached duty), of Hill's division. The 24th and the 7th Virginia, except their skirmishers, did not pull a trigger, but were under the fire of the artillery and partly that of infantry. Nor did the 18th North Carolina take part in the battle.

From the best information I have been able to obtain, from the official reports and otherwise, I fix the number of Confederates in this battle against General Burnside's 13,083 men as follows:

Jenkins' brigade	500
Garnett's brigade	250
Drayton's brigade (51st Ga. & 15th S.C. Regmts.)	200
Kemper's brigade	300
Toombs' brigade (including Maj. Little's bat., 140)	<u>600</u>
Total Jones' Division	1850
A. P. Hill's three brigades, less 18th North Carolina, detached	<u>1900</u>
Total, both divisions	3750

Casualties—General Jones reports, including the battle of Boonsboro, 1435. Toombs' brigade was not at Boonsboro, and the brigade commanded by Colonel Geo. T. Anderson was detached in the early morning, and we have no reports from the 28th Virginia regiment of Garnett's brigade, and only in part from Toombs' regiments, and but from one regiment of Kemper's. Approximately, however, the losses were as follows:

Col. Walker, commanding brigade of Jenkins, reports	210
Taking 4 regiments of Garnett's and	80

averaging the 5th

Drayton's two regiments, estimated	100
Kemper's regiments, estimated	160
Toombs, stated	<u>346</u>
Total	996

The disparity in numbers on this part of the field was probably greater than on any other—nearly three and a half to one.

There has been, and probably will always be, uncertainty as to the number of men General Lee had in the battle of Sharpsburg. Colonel Taylor, of the staff of General Lee, and Adjutant General of the army, puts the number at 35,250—including cavalry and artillery, putting the infantry force at 27,255. This is surely incorrect for the reasons: first, that the returns of the army on the 20th of July, 1862, a few days before the movement of the army to North Virginia from Richmond began, show the total cavalry 3740. In the second place the fact is well known that the cavalry and artillery had been engaged in the battle of Cedar Run, the battles around Manassas, and at South Mountain, Harper's Ferry, Crampton's Pass, and Boonsboro, and the losses must have been large; and again, there were only three brigades of Confederate cavalry at Sharpsburg—Lee's, Hampton's and Robertson's, the latter under Munford, and there is no evidence that either of the two latter named fired a shot at Sharpsburg. Lee's brigade could not have numbered more than a third of the cavalry force, say 1500—a liberal estimate—and the artillerists 1800. We have 3300. A careful examination of all the sources of information available to me, including official reports, and my own personal knowledge and observation on the march and on the field, inclines me strongly to the opinion and belief that the Confederate troops on the field of Sharpsburg on the firing line and actually engaged on the 17th of September numbered:

Jackson's division	1600
Ewell's division	3400
D. H. Hill's division	3000
D. R. Jones' division	1850
A. P. Hill's division	1900
Hood's division	2000

McLaws' division	2893
R. H. Anderson's division	3500
J. G. Walker's division	3200
Geo. T. Anderson's brigade	300
N. G. Evans' division	1500
Lee's cavalry brigade	1500
Artillerists	1800
Total	28,443

Note:—There is no evidence that Armistead's brigade of R. H. Anderson's division drew trigger in this battle.

The Confederate casualties in the Maryland campaign as given in the War Records	13,609
The Federal casualties, including the garrison at Harper's Ferry	27,767
Deducting the Harper's Ferry garrison, we have the Federal losses of the campaign	15,203
Deducting Federal losses at Boonsboro Gap of 1813, Crampton's Gap 533, we have approximately as the Federal loss in battle of Sharpsburg	12,856
Deducting the estimated Confederate loss at Boonsboro Gap, Crampton's Gap and Harper's Ferry, 3948, from the campaign loss, we have approximately as the Confederate loss at Sharpsburg	9,661

The actual number of Union soldiers on the firing line in the battle of Sharpsburg could not have exceeded 68,000 men, but Porter's corps, some

19,000, was close up in the center in reserve, with more than 14,000, only a march away.

The night of the battle several of our men went out on the battlefield, to look after the dead and wounded and for other purposes. Among those from my company who went out in this way were Travis Burton and Lieutenant Stone, who shortly returned with an unwounded prisoner of a Rhode Island regiment, who had failed to get away with his retreating comrades. This prisoner was a mere boy, who exhibited considerable signs of fear and trepidation, and with whom Captain Ashby had quite a little fun.

On passing over a battlefield after the close of the battle, it will usually be observed that the pockets of the dead, and sometimes of the wounded, have been turned out. A soldier will generally take from the battlefield and the dead what he wants.

The next day, the 18th, was in the main quiet, with some little picket firing; the wounded were being cared for and the dead buried. In the immediate front of our brigade, some fifty yards away, the farthest point reached by Harland's Federal brigade the day before, and the ground on which it stood, when charged by the brigades of Toombs and Kemper, I counted the bodies of 33 dead Union soldiers of the 8th Connecticut regiment. One of the wounded was still living, to whom I gave a drink of water and filled his canteen. During the day a man of our regiment, who had gone forward to help remove the Federal wounded, was shot through the body and killed by a Federal sharpshooter, who was so far away that the report from his rifle was not heard by the men engaged in the removal of the wounded.

On the night of the 18th, we left the battle line, moving to the Potomac, wading the river at the ford near Sheperdstown, and instead of singing when crossing the river thirteen days before, "Maryland, MY Maryland!" the song was, "Carry me back, oh! carry me back to old Virginia, once more."

A halt was made some three miles from the river; moving in a day or two to near Bunker Hill, and again to a point nearer to Winchester, close by a large spring, where we received quite a number of accessions to our ranks by the return of the shoeless, sick, and some wounded men left along the route of our advance into Maryland.

---

[4]

The headlong rush of Archer's brigade across the front of the 7th Virginia regiment prevented its firing into the enemy.

CHAPTER XV

- **From Winchester to Culpeper.**

- **Reorganization of the Army.**

- **What Happened at Culpeper.**

- **To Fredericksburg and Battle There.**

- **In Winter Quarters.**

- **Incidents of the Camp.**

Longstreet's command left the vicinity of Winchester the latter part of October, 1862, crossing the Shenandoah river, Blue Ridge, and reaching Culpeper the early part of the first week in November, going into camp a short distance southeast of the court house. Several companies of the 7th regiment were from Orange, Culpeper, Madison and Rappahannock, and while in this camp the friends of these men came with wagons loaded with provisions and clothing, supplying many of their needs, and relieving much of their suffering.

Here the reorganization of the army was effected into two army corps, the first commanded by General James Longstreet, the second by General Thomas J. (Stonewall) Jackson. Later a third corps was organized, of which Lieutenant General A. P. Hill was appointed commander. Pickett's division was also organized, composed of five brigades, as follows:

- First brigade, General James L. Kemper: regiments 1st, 3d, 7th, 11th and 24th Virginia.

-

- Second brigade, General R. B. Garnett: regiments 8th, 18th, 19th, 28th and 56th Virginia.

-

- Third brigade, General Lewis A. Armistead: regiments 9th, 14th, 38th, 53d and 57th Virginia.

-

- Fourth brigade, General M. D. Corse: regiments 15th, 17th, 29th, 30th and 32d Virginia.

-

- These four Virginia brigades were composed of the flower of the state.

-

- Jenkins' South Carolina brigade—General M. Jenkins: regiments Palmetto sharpshooters, 1st, 2d, 3d, 4th, 5th and 6th South Carolina, and 4th battalion.

-

- To which was attached the following Virginia artillery: Major Dearing's 38th battalion, with Caskie's, Stribling's and Latham's batteries.

Many additions were made to the ranks at Culpeper, greatly increasing our strength; the organization now being better as to numbers and discipline than at any previous period. The health of the soldiers was also much improved; the entire army, however, still being deficient in equipment, especially shoes, overcoats and blankets, and the chilly November winds, the precursor of that fearfully cold winter just ahead, causing suffering among the men, who bore the same without murmuring—such was their metal. The weather by this time had become quite cold, the men building strong fires, and to keep off the cold ground at night they procured, when possible, two or three flat fence rails, placing them near the fire, lying down upon them. Such was their feather bed, covering themselves with a blanket if they chanced to have one.

Here the writer was appointed Sergeant-Major of the regiment, succeeding Sergeant-Major Park, disabled in the second battle of Manassas—an honor as proud as anything that has come to him since.

The march to Fredericksburg began November 18, over the old plank road, passing through the Wilderness and Chancellorsville, soon to be drenched in blood in the most famous battles of the war—Chancellorsville, Wilderness and Spottsylvania. Here it may be said that in the County of Spottsylvania more important battles were fought, more blood shed and more men killed and wounded, and more soldiers lie buried, than in any other county in the United States. Here were fought the first and second battles of Fredericksburg, Chancellorsville, the two days Wilderness, and the series of battles in and around Spottsylvania court house, including countless skirmishes and cavalry combats. It is no exaggeration to say that the men killed and wounded in the battles, skirmishes and combats in the county reached 100,000.

When we reached the vicinity of Fredericksburg, snow had fallen to the depth of two inches or so, which had to be cleared off to find a dry place to go to bed. Here we remained for twenty or more days, performing no guard duty, but kept busy gathering fuel to make fires to keep warm. Eating our rations gave us little trouble, not nearly so much as when or where the next would come from. The men smoked, some croaked—for it must be remarked that in the army there are chronic grumblers, who complain of short rations, continually saying the war would never end; others that we were going to be whipped in the next fight; but men of this class were few in number, the greater part in good spirits, buoyant with hope and confident of the final triumph of our cause.

At early dawn, December 11, we stood to arms, continuing to do so until early Saturday morning, the 13th, two days and nights, then moving out from camp in the direction of the Rappahannock. The two days' suspense just alluded to proved a severe task on the staying powers of the strongest men. Our march now continued until we reached a point overlooking the river valley. Although frosty, the air bracing, a dense fog hovered pall-like over the valley below, shutting off from our view the enemy, now in full force along the river, and the broad bottom land at our feet. As the sun broke away the fog, the movement continuing, there was heard to our left occasional rattle of musketry. Meeting a negro man loaded with blankets, canteens, haversacks and general baggage, puffing as if almost out of breath, with great drops of sweat as big as peas on his face—someone said to him: "Hello, Uncle! Where are you going?"

His answer was, "To de r'ar, Sah!"

Then the query, "To what command do you belong?"

"Barksdale's brigade, Sah."

"Is it running, too?"

"No, boss, it never runs, but I always do."

By this time the fog had so lifted that we could see in front far to our right the gleam of a long line of bayonets, though we could not see the men who held the guns. We halted on the break of the heights, where we witnessed the combat between the Federal and Confederate skirmishers of Jackson's command, as well also as the assault by a part of the Federal line of battle against Jackson's men, and the repulse of the Federals. Not being longer permitted to enjoy the further progress of the battle on that part of the field, we were now hastened down the hill and formed in line of battle in a wood with an open field in front; the fog, however, still bothered in seeing the game we were watching. The dictates of self preservation impelled us to throw up some rude breastworks, which would furnish fair protection from rifle or musket balls, but none from artillery fire. While in this position, where we remained until the middle of the afternoon, there could be heard the commands of the officers of the enemy quite as distinctly as those of our own.

Many of the men without overcoats and thinly clad stood shivering from the cold fog, their beards white with frost. General Kemper came along and made a patriotic, soul-stirring speech, which had a good effect upon the men, also making similar speeches to other regiments of the brigade.

The Confederates on the left at the foot of Marye's Hill being heavily pressed, our brigade was withdrawn and pushed across the hills and valleys to a position in rear and easy supporting distance of the troops holding position at the foot of the hill. While in this new position, the musket and rifle balls of the enemy flew thick and fast, a number being wounded, among them Lewis N. Wiley, of D company, one ball striking the writer's left foot, which had become so hard by going without shoes that but little injury was inflicted. At dark and as the last charge of the enemy was repulsed, our brigade moved forward, relieving some Georgia and North Carolina troops; the left of my regiment resting on the road leading out of Fredericksburg over the hill, and extending to the right on the upper side of a road leaving the last named road at right angles; occupying the angle made by these roads, where we lay down on the upper side of the road on a wall made by a stone fence built against the foot of the hill, which afforded us no protection.

The 1st Virginia regiment was on our right and in line in the road and behind the stone fence; the men of our regiment, with bayonets, boards, sticks and tin cups, went to work to cut a trench on top of the wall on which it lay, and by daylight the next morning had made themselves works sufficient to protect them against minnie balls.

Around us lay the Confederate dead, two dead Georgians lying in the midst of my company, by whose side the writer lay down and slept. The night was cool, but not cold; there was no moon, but bright starlight, to which, for several hours, was added the Aurora borealis. About midnight I was aroused by Captain Bane, who said to me, "They are coming," and with my ear to the ground I could distinctly hear hoof strokes approaching from the direction of the city. In a moment every man was at his post, musket in hand; dead stillness reigned. The mounted parties rode up to the intersection of the roads and were captured by the first regiment. The party consisted of three Federal officers, one a member of General Hooker's staff. They had ridden forward to examine their skirmish line and had been allowed to pass through unchallenged, finding themselves in a trap. They were sent under guard to the provost-marshal in charge of an Irish sergeant and guard of the 1st Virginia. This sergeant on his return next morning, while passing our company, was severely wounded by a Federal sharpshooter standing behind the corner of a brick house a hundred yards or more away.

We had been advised on the night of the battle that the attack was expected to be renewed the next morning, in view of which we had been furnished with one hundred rounds of ammunition, with instructions to hold the position at all hazards, that we would be supported by a line of battle on the hill in our rear. The attack was not made, though we remained in position during the day and night, skirmishing and sharpshooting. Next day after the battle, while holding the line in front of Fredericksburg, some of our boys carried water to the Federal wounded lying in our front, though at the risk of life.

Amid a rainstorm on the night of the 14th, the enemy stole away and crossed the river. The battle over and the danger past, we retired to our camp on the hills south of Fredericksburg, where we remained for nearly two months, suffering much from cold, want of clothing and shoes; many of the barefooted men making and wearing rawhide moccasins. Frequently, to prevent suffering at night, the men made log fires and in evening rolled away the burning logs, cleared away the fire and ashes and made their sleeping places on the warm earth from which the fire had been removed. When we had snow, the men would fight snowball battles, in which frequently someone was seriously hurt. We did little picket or guard duty, and many engaged in card playing. Religious exercises were now infrequent. I recall going once to divine services, when the Chaplain, Mr. McCarthy, preached; and I remember to this good day the text which formed the basis of his discourse. It was from the 53d chapter of Isaiah, verse i: "Who hath believed our report? and to whom is the arm of the Lord revealed?"

During the long, dreary, cold two months following the battle of Fredericksburg, while in camp amid privations and suffering, the men discussed freely the questions touching the war, its conduct, and prospects for peace. The soldiers talked gravely of these matters, discussing them frequently with much earnestness, not a few becoming homesick and longing for the termination of the game of conflict and death. An ever abiding confidence in our cause, its justness, and our belief in the final triumph of right over wrong coupled with invincible spirits ever ready to brave the storm of battle, caused our sufferings and hardships to be treated as trivial, as compared with the issue at stake. The end, however, was not yet in sight, and little did we dream that it would be reached as it was; for while it was supposed that the private soldier knew little of what was transpiring throughout the country—North, South or in Europe, yet it is a fact that the questions of resources of the South in men and supplies; the North with its vast resources, with the old world to draw upon for men to fight its battles, were frequently talked of, as well as the remote possibility of foreign intervention; its effect upon the war; the peace feeling North, and its probable effect. Our confidence in the armies of the Confederacy, and our ability to successfully resist the Federal armies with their overwhelming numbers was scarcely doubted. It was remarkable what confidence the men reposed in General Lee; they were ready to follow him wherever he might lead, or order them to go.

In company D was one, Dan East, who was never in a battle, and never intended to be; yet Dan knew more about it than anyone who had gone through it; always turning up after the battle with a full haversack, good blanket, overcoat and shoes. As usual, Dan walked into the camp after the battle of Fredericksburg, when the Colonel determined to punish him; he caused a placard with the word "Coward" in large letters to be fastened across his back, and with rail on his shoulder he was marched to and fro in front of the regiment; but this had little effect on Dan, and the first opportunity he helped himself to a fellow soldier's clothing and other goods, which were found in his quarters. The men of the company decided to rid the service of Dan by whipping him out of it, which they did.

It was while in this camp that a rencounter occurred between Hight and Young, both large, stout, athletic men, pretty equally matched in size, strength and good mettle. The fight was as close as two brave men could make it, but friends intervened and the combatants were separated.

Let us now return to the result of the battle of Fredericksburg, as far as forces engaged and casualties suffered are concerned.

The Federal army in this battle numbered 50,000; casualties, 12,653. Confederate army, 20,000; casualties, 4201. Casualties in Kemper's brigade, 46; in 7th Virginia regiment, 5; in Co. D, 1; Lewis N. Wiley, wounded—with the whack taken at the writer's foot, already described.

January 20, 1863, the command was suddenly called to arms, marched up the Rappahannock in the direction of Banks' ford, where, it was reported, the Federal army was threatening to cross the river. We remained out one night in the snow, rain, mud and slush, returning to camp next day.

CHAPTER XVI

- Leaving Camp.

- March Through Spottsylvania.

- Louisa.

- Hanover, Petersburg.

- First North Carolina Campaign.

- Heavy Snowfall and Battle.

- Accident to Anderson Meadows Near Chester.

- Camp Near Petersburg.

- Gardner Exchanges Hats.

- Lieutenant Stone in a Box.

- To Weldon, Goldsboro and Kinston.

- At Suffolk, Virginia. Return via Petersburg, Chester, Richmond, to Taylorsville.

- John, the Drummer Boy.

- Professor Hughes, Frank Burrows and Others.

- Across the Pamunkey, Return Taylorsville and to Culpeper.

Monday, February 16, 1863, in the midst of a storm of snow and sleet, Pickett's division took up its line of march heading toward Richmond. Reports were rife relating to destination, some saying Charleston, others Savannah or Blackwater; all were on the list of probabilities, the line of march being through the counties of Spottsylvania, Louisa and Hanover. At Hanover Junction Sergeant A. L. Fry, who had returned from captivity, rejoined us. Within eight miles or so of Richmond the moving army went into camp, resting a few days from fatiguing march, then proceeding through Richmond to Chester station on the Richmond and Petersburg railroad.

The brave Lieutenant-Colonel Flowerree of the 7th regiment, having imbibed a little freely, as we passed through Richmond was placed in arrest, charged with the breach of soldierly good conduct. He was finally restored to us on the return from Gettysburg; a streak of luck that saved the Colonel from being in the great battle.

The day of our arrival at Chester was cool, the early night was clear, the sky blue, the stars shining—nothing that betokened any sudden change of weather. Awakening next morning we found we had a blanket of snow twelve inches deep—the men lying in rows reminding one of a cemetery, and on rising, of the resurrection day. We soon built roaring fires and went out and fought a great snowball battle. The explosion of cartridges in a cartridge box that had been hung up too near the fire came near costing Anderson Meadows the loss of his eyes. Meadows was quite a remarkable man. When he went into the army he could neither read nor write, but during the service he became quite proficient in all, was a number one cook and a brave soldier, surviving the war.

Our next move took us to a point about a mile southeast of Petersburg, where we went into camp. The weather had somewhat moderated, but snow still on the ground. Our Lieutenant Stone, who had been home on furlough, returned to us here. The camp was always more lively when he was present, for there was no fun or mischief started in which he did not make a full hand, and in the army anything that cultivates cheerfulness is of real value. Many of the men went into Petersburg, some without leave, among them Gardner of Company D, who, on his return, was discovered wearing a good looking hat instead of the old, dingy cap he had worn away. Inquiry being made as to how he became possessed of the hat, he replied: "I swapped with a fellow—but he wasn't there!"

March 25 a shift was made to the Weldon and Petersburg railway station, and while the train to carry us south was being made ready, some of the men took on too many drinks, our jolly Lieutenant Stone being one, and becoming boisterous, fell into the hands of the city police. To keep our Lieutenant out of their clutches, the men of the company put him in a box car, fastening the doors, but as he did not fancy being a prisoner in a box car he kicked off one of the doors, coming out with it, hanging as he came on a nail or part of the door, the leg of his trousers catching the same a little above the knee, tearing one leg of his trousers.

Next morning found us at Weldon, where we remained several hours, and while here Pat Wood, an Irishman of the 1st regiment, started some kind of a row, which brought General Ransom, the commandant of the post, upon the scene, and which resulted in a peremptory order for the whole command to move on, which it did. Crowded into box cars, without fire, the weather cold, the result cold feet and general discomfort. But a soldier equal to almost any emergency, especially where his personal safety and comfort are concerned, and determining to have fires, covered the floor of each car with sand. On this fires were made of longleaf North Carolina pine. The smoke was dense, and, having no escape, settled upon the men, so that when Goldsboro was reached that evening we were thought to belong to the "colored brigade."

Next day we proceeded about twenty-five miles to Kinston, on the Neuse river, about thirty-five miles west from Newbern. From Kinston we did some scouting and picket duty on the roads leading to Newbern, the object seeming to be to keep the enemy at Newbern close in, while our commissariat gathered supplies, as General Longstreet with Hood's division was likewise doing at Suffolk, Va. The enemy had occupied Kinston the preceding winter, and many of the houses had been destroyed; the inhabitants had removed, either inside the Union military lines, or to the interior of the state. The village, in fact, was entirely deserted.

Our brigade left Kinston April 9, moving by rail to Goldsboro and Weldon to a point twenty or more miles south of Petersburg, from whence we marched through the Blackwater region—the counties of Southampton, its county town Jerusalem, Isle of Wight—to the neighborhood of Suffolk in Nausemond County, where we united with the division of General Hood, then closely investing the town.

I will here relate two incidents occurring on our journey to and from Kinston. While halting at Goldsboro, a soldier of Company F, 24th Virginia, named Adams, went to a pie stand kept by an old lady, took part of her pies and was walking away without paying therefor, when he was arrested by a town policeman, whom the soldier sought to resist, and in the fight Adams was killed. The other incident was, as we were being transported by the railway in box cars between Kinston and Goldsboro, a part of the men were on top of the boxes, and along portions of the railway were overhead bridges for the accommodation of travelers on the county roads. One, Manly Reece of Co. G, 24th Virginia, standing erect on one of the box cars, and not observing an overhead bridge, was struck, knocked from the car and killed.

At Suffolk lively skirmishing was kept up for quite a while, sometimes approaching a battle. While here we were formed into line of battle to receive the foe, but he did not come. Matters thus continued until we retired, as hereinafter related.

From a letter I wrote to a friend dated April 25 (the original furnished while writing these pages), it appears we reached Suffolk the 12th of the month. I state in the letter: "This is the 13th day that we have been in close proximity to the enemy." While at Suffolk three of my Company D—Hugh J. Wilburn, James H. Gardner and John S. W. French, deserted to the enemy.

Having accomplished the object of the expedition, the troops quietly withdrew from the front a little after dark on the evening of Monday, May

4. On reaching South Quay, we heard of the great Confederate victory at Chancellorsville. Pushing ahead through Petersburg to Chester Station, we again halted there for a few days for rest and recuperation. While here in camp, Isaac Hare and Travis Burton of Company D took "French furlough" and joined themselves to a portion of the Confederate army serving in southwestern Virginia. The cause of this action was never explained.

Baldwin L. Hoge, in handling a knife, accidentally wounded himself in the knee, was sent to the hospital, and was not able for field service for several months.

It was here also that the men of the divisions of Pickett and Hood heard with sorrow of the death of General Stonewall Jackson, an irreparable loss; for his place could not well be filled, and it seemed that with his loss our cause began to wane. The humblest private in all the armies of the South deeply mourned the loss of this Christian man and able general.

Hood's Texans were encamped across the railroad from us, amusing themselves by putting musket caps on the rails just in advance of the approach of a passenger train, then taking their stand close beside the track, bushes or brush in hand. On the caps exploding, the passengers would put their heads out of the windows to ascertain the cause of the popping, and found on drawing their heads back into the coach that they were hatless—a slick trick of the soldiers to get for themselves a supply of hats.

Resuming the line of march May 12, we passed through Richmond to Taylorsville in Hanover County, not far from the Junction, the crossing of the Virginia Central over the Richmond, Fredericksburg and Potomac railroad.

A series of religious meetings were here held and many professed faith in Christ, the writer among the number. From a letter to a friend at home, dated at Taylorsville, May 26, I see that I stated: "We are now resting from our hard marches, which, however, may be resumed at any time. There is a religious meeting going on here now. Rev. Dr. Pryor of Petersburg is preaching for us. I think he will be able to do great good. Nearly every man in the brigade seems to take an interest in the meetings. I hope that much good may be done. Our soldiers are loyal to their country, and Oh! how grand if they would only be loyal to God."

In the interim of our arrival at Taylorsville and leaving there, the division took a journey across the Pamunkey into King and Queen County, returning to Taylorsville. A few days thereafter we had division review, being drawn up in line to receive General Pickett, to whom, as he passed by, we were to lower the flags and present arms, the drums to beat. John

Whitlock was the drummer boy for our regiment, a little waif picked up in Richmond by some one of our regimental band or drum corps, of which Professor Hughes was leader, with Frank Burrows and others members of the band. John Whitlock was a mischievous boy, who, to keep from beating the drum, would lose or throw away the sticks; so when on this review he was ordered by the Colonel to beat the drum, there was no response, on account of which, on return to camp, I was ordered to place on John a drum shirt, which consisted of taking the heads out of the drum and slipping the barrel down over his arms. John cried and begged, and I let him go upon his promise to do better in the future.

At Taylorsville Pickett's division, fully equipped, was made ready for the most active field service. The ranks were recuperated by those who had been sick, those recovered from wounds, as well as by recruits, and all vacancies in the officers of the line and staff, among them Captain John H. Parr, who had been appointed Adjutant to fill the vacancy occasioned by the death of Adjutant Starke, killed in the battle of Frazier's Farm. Company D had lost up to this time, killed in battle, died of wounds, disease, transfers to other commands, detached service and desertion, nearly 70 men; had received no recruits except those received in August, 1861, and some were sick and in hospital.

It is probable we left Taylorsville for Culpeper June 3, as I see from a letter written by me on the 11th of June from a point about eight miles from Culpeper court house, that I say: "We have been marching for the last eight days, have now halted eight miles from Culpeper court house. Our cavalry had a severe fight with the enemy day before yesterday. I think we are to have a hard summer's campaign. It is reported that the Yankees have moved back to Manassas and Bull Run. There has been some fighting at Fredericksburg, where some of the enemy have crossed and are throwing up fortifications."

It was our custom to call the enemy Yankees; some said "D—d Yankees," and they likewise called us "D—d rebels," neither side meaning any offense, nor the expression carrying any personal ill will. It is told by General Sherman in his Atlanta, or some other campaign, that he heard an old negro praying, saying among other things, "Oh! Lord, bless the d—d Yankees." We used the word Yankee, prior to the war, applying it to the New England people, the descendants of the Puritans, the people whose ancestors landed on Plymouth Rock, of whom General Early is credited with saying, "If that rock had landed on them, we would never have had the d—d h—l fired war." The word Yankee is of uncertain derivation though said to be an Indian corruption of the French word, Anglais, meaning English. The Union soldiers usually called us "Johnnies," or "Johnny Rebs."

The army had been organized with three corps—first, Longstreet's; second, Ewell's, and third, A. P. Hill's. While at Culpeper, where the Confederate army was being mobilized, additional numbers were being received into the ranks. The passionate ardor of our people for their country's cause had brought to the army nearly every man fit for the service. It was perhaps the largest efficient number of men, and composed of the best fighting material that General Lee ever led to battle. Most of the men were well inured to the service, and well prepared to undergo the greatest privations and hardships; and by this time most of the cowards and skulkers had either gotten out of the army or had never gotten in, or gone over to the enemy. In these men General Lee imposed the utmost confidence, and this confidence was reciprocated. It is stated upon authority that as the army went forward on its march to Pennsylvania, while passing through the valley of Virginia not far from Berryville, near which General Lee had stopped and dined with a friend, that in the act of mounting his horse to depart, his host remarked: "I have never had any confidence in the success of our cause till now I see our army marching north." Promptly came General Lee's only reply: "Doctor, there marches the finest body of men that ever tramped the earth."

The usual order to cook rations and prepare to move at a moment's notice was given, and everything was put in readiness; the camp was all bustle and confusion.

CHAPTER XVII

- **Pennsylvania Campaign of July, 1863.**

- **Culpeper and Snicker's Gap.**

- **Fording the Potomac.**

- **Shooting a Deserter.**

- **Pennsylvania Invaded.**

- **Chambersburg.**

- **My Dream.**

- **Willoughby Run.**

- **Roll Call.**

I am now about to record the things I saw in connection with the greatest endeavor of the Army of Northern Virginia during the Civil War, which led up to the Battle of Gettysburg, a campaign which startled the North, alarmed the capital at Washington, and inspired General Lee's army with new heroism and courage. We were going to Pennsylvania in part to procure that for which Jacob's sons went down into Egypt.

Monday, June 15, 1863, the head of the column moved out, directed toward the Blue Ridge and Snicker's Gap, through which we passed June 20, crossing the Shenandoah River at Castleman's ferry, where we were detained three or four days, and again at Berryville, for the purpose of keeping in supporting distance of our cavalry operating against that of the enemy east of the Ridge. The march from Culpeper was conducted left in front, the enemy being on our right. The Confederate cavalry had for several days been engaged with that of the enemy in the vicinity of Aldie and Upperville. The army was followed by a large drove of beef cattle, James B. Croy, of Company D, being detailed as one of the drivers, thereby escaping the storm at Gettysburg.

The way for the march of the army through the Virginia valley had been cleared by Ewell's corps, which had defeated and driven away the Federal troops at Winchester and Martinsburg; while the Confederate cavalry had cut and destroyed a portion of the Baltimore & Ohio railroad west of Harper's Ferry, and Jenkins' Confederate cavalry brigade had crossed the Potomac, entering Maryland and Pennsylvania. The weather was hot and the march continued through Martinsburg by Falling Waters, crossing the

Potomac by wading to Williamsport, Md., going into camp a short distance out of the town. Here it was late in the evening that a deserter from the 18th Virginia regiment was executed by shooting.

The morale of the army was superb, officers and men alike inspired with confidence in the ability of the army to beat its old antagonist anywhere he chose to meet us. We were moving into the enemy's country in fine spirit— no straggling, no desertion, no destruction of private property, no outrages committed upon non-combatants, the orders of the commanding general on this subject being strictly observed. Among the men were expressions of disapproval of the invasion of the North. We had uniformly insisted upon defensive warfare on our own soil; in other words, we steadfastly contended against the claim of the enemy to invade our own land, and logically we should be bound by the same reasoning. However, in the last analysis every man in the army of Northern Virginia was loyal to his commander-in-chief, wherever he should lead. Here, indeed, was a spectacle: An army of more than sixty thousand freemen, every man a soldier in the true sense of the word, brave, resolute, fearless, the heroes and victors of many fields, marching unobstructed and thus far unopposed through an enemy's country, whose people had scarcely known that war was in progress; living in quiet and plenty. The march was continued with steady tread to Hagerstown, where a halt was made to allow Hill's corps, which had crossed the river below, to pass. Again marching, the Cumberland Valley in Pennsylvania was entered, a magnificent land, the counterpart of the lovely valley of Virginia, the sight bringing homesickness to the heart of not a few Virginia boys. Nothing was seen indicating that these people knew that a terrible war had been raging for two years, only a few miles away; certain it is they had felt little of its effect, either upon their population or resources. At Greencastle was noted among the people defiance and vindictive mien; while not speaking out, their looks indicated that deep down in their bosoms was rancor and the wish that all the rebel hosts were dead and corralled by the devil.

Saturday, June 27, Chambersburg, the capital—county town—of Franklin County, was entered by our column; passing to the outskirts on the north, or northwest side thereof, halting in the street in front of a beautiful residence, said to be that of Colonel McClure. Some ladies appeared and volunteered to deliver a sharp, spicy address, which was responded to by the band of our regiment, with "Dixie." The boys sang "Dixie" and "Bonnie Blue Flag," laughed and cheered lustily, then marched on a few miles on the York road and went into camp.

Pickett's division was left at Chambersburg to guard the trains until General Imboden's command could close up and relieve it, which it did on the evening of July 1. While waiting to be relieved, the men of Pickett's division were employed in tearing up the track of the Cumberland Valley railroad, which was thoroughly done for a mile or more, piling and firing the ties, heating the rails and bending them around trees.

During the march from the Potomac to Chambersburg, I one night had a dream in which I saw my left shoulder mangled by a cannon shot and I lying on the battlefield bleeding, dying. This dream, not like many not recollected, deeply impressed itself upon my mind, and I found myself unable to throw it off. When three days later in the battle at Gettysburg I was struck by an exploding shell on my left side, the dream instantly came up, and I said, here now is its fulfillment. Other soldiers, like myself, probably during and after the war dreamed of being in battle, hearing distinctly the booming of cannon, the noise of bursting shell and the rattle of musketry.

About 2 o'clock on Thursday morning, July 2, being aroused by the sound of the long roll, we were quickly in line, the column moving on the road leading to Gettysburg. The march was rapid, and unceasing, until we reached the vicinity of the coming conflict at Gettysburg, a distance of twenty-five miles or more over a dusty road, beneath a burning July sun, passing on the way the smoldering ruins of Thad Stevens' iron furnace, which had been fired by General J. A. Early a few days before. The other divisions of our corps (Longstreet's) had preceded us some twenty-four hours, arriving in time to make the principal battle of the second day.

On the march over South Mountain, reaching the east side, passing through the small hamlets of Cashtown and Seven Stars, plainly could be heard the roar of Longstreet's battle of that evening. Near the middle of the afternoon the division halted at Willoughby Run, two miles from Gettysburg; the men soon scattered, some getting water, some eating and some in conversation. As the shades of night began to gather on this bright eve, being fatigued with the day's march, all retired early to rest, little dreaming that upon such lovely eve, such awful morn should rise. Brave, happy souls, little do you anticipate the horrors of the next twenty-four hours! All was quiet during the night until reveille, which was sounded before day, when we fell into ranks for roll call, the last for so many gallant men, who on this eventful day were to pour out their life's blood for freedom and the right, as God gave them to see the right, and to go to that bourne from whence no traveler returns.

CHAPTER XVIII

- **Finishing Roll Call.**

- **March to the Field.**

- **Inspection of Arms.**

- **Fearful Artillery Duel.**

- **The Charge.**

- **Killed and Wounded.**

- **Army Retires.**

- **Crosses the Potomac.**

Proceeding with the roll call, the officers and men of Company D were: Captain R. H. Bane, Lieutenants E. M. Stone, John W. Mullins and E. R. Walker; non-commissioned, Sergeants T. S. Taylor, W. H. H. Snidow, the writer; Corporals A. J. Thompson, Daniel Bish, George C. Mullins, J. B. Young; Privates Akers, Barrett, Crawford, Darr, Fortner (J. H.), Fortner (W. C.), Hight, Hurt (J. J.), Jones, Lewy (Jo), Meadows (Anderson), Meadows (John), Minnich, Munsey, Peters, Sarver (D. L.), Sublett, Stafford, Wilburn (G. L.) and Wilburn (W. I.). Total, 31, being all of Company D present that I recall. I believe this to be correct.

James B. Croy had been detailed to drive beef cattle; Alexander Bolton belonged to the ambulance corps, and Charles A. Hale was company cook. During the terrific artillery duel, which followed, Captain Bane and Lieutenant Mullins were prostrated by heat, from which they did not recover for some days. Lieutenant Stone had been assigned to the command of Company E of the regiment, which had no commissioned officer present. Lieutenant Walker was left in command of our company, and just as the artillery duel was about closing, and but a few minutes before the general advance began, I was knocked out of ranks by a bursting shell, of which more later. The company therefore went into the charge with but 28 men, counting Lieutenant Stone leading Company E, and Young, color guard. The three brigades of Pickett's division present were Garnett's, Kemper's and Armistead's, composed of fifteen Virginia regiments, numbering in the aggregate that morning about 4,700 men, which included the General's staff, and regimental officers, of which there was the full complement; Colonel W. Tazewell Patton, commanding the 7th Virginia regiment, being the only field officer of the regiment then present. The division, from the major-general down, was composed of Virginians, many of them mere boys, and the probability is that the average age of the men in the ranks, including the line officers, did not exceed 19 years. I had just passed my eighteenth birthday. In the division were companies from the counties of Bedford, Campbell, Franklin, Patrick, Henry, Floyd, Montgomery, Pulaski, Giles, Craig, Mercer, Madison, Orange, Culpeper, Rappahannock, Greene, Albemarle, Carroll, Appomattox, Pittsylvania, Prince Edward, Norfolk, Nansemond, and others; and from the cities of Richmond, Lynchburg, Norfolk and Portsmouth—volunteers all, many of them school boys who had entered the service at the commencement of the war, and becoming fully inured to the service.

Our brigade, commanded by the gallant and impetuous General James L. Kemper, was in front during the morning's march, and as we formed into battle line held the right, Garnett's brigade on the left, Armistead's a little to the left and rear. The line was formed as early as 7 o'clock A.M. Inspection of arms was had and everything put in readiness for the engagement then imminent. We moved out of a skirt of woods, went forward a short distance into a field, on which was standing a crop of rye not yet harvested. Our position was now on Seminary Ridge, four hundred yards or so back from the top, under the crest; the line formed somewhat obliquely to the Emmitsburg road in front of us, with the Confederate batteries on the crest four hundred yards or more in front of us. Pickett's division was to lead the assault, the wings supported on the right by Wilcox's brigade, Heth's division under General Pettigrew, supported by the brigades of Scales and Lane, under General Trimble, for the purpose of supporting the left: all obstructions cleared away from the immediate front.

In the formation thus made, arms were stacked and we, with the understanding that when two signal guns were fired, to take arms and lie flat on the ground. All along the Confederate front was massed our artillery, perhaps 75 or more guns. The Federal artillery, 220 guns, along their whole front. The lines of the two armies, now held as by a leash, were 1,430 yards from each other, the distance between the opposing batteries an average of a little more than 1,000 yards. The Federal guns exceeded ours in number and quality of metal.

Now the suspense was something awful. The men were grave and thoughtful, but showed no signs of fear. The multitude awaiting judgment could not be more seriously impressed with what was now about to follow. However, a soldier in the field rarely thought his time to die had exactly arrived—that is, it would be the other fellow's time—and well it was so. Occasionally a man was met who had made up his mind that the next battle would be his last. Men have been known to have such presentiment and sure enough be killed in the next engagement. Such was true of our gallant Colonel Patton, who yielded up his promising young life in this battle.

The issue of the campaign and of the Civil War itself, as history shows, was now trembling in the balance. Victory or defeat to either side would be in effect a settlement of the issues involved; this the officers and men seemed clearly to realize. Under such conditions all were impatient of the restraint. To the brave soldier going into battle, knowing he must go, the moments seem to lengthen. This feeling is not born of his love for fighting, but it is rather the nervous anxiety to determine the momentous issue as quickly as possible, without stopping to count the cost, realizing if it must be done, "it were well it were done quickly." Over-confidence pervaded the Confederate army, from the commanding general down to the shakiest private in the ranks. Too much over-confidence was the bane of our battle. For more than six long hours the men were waiting, listening for the sound of the signal guns. The stillness was at last broken: the shot was fired: down, according to program, went the men on their faces.

Now began the most terrible artillery duel that beyond question ever took place on the American continent, or, the writer believes, anywhere else. Never had a storm so dreadful burst upon mortal man. The atmosphere was rent and broken by the rush and crash of projectiles—solid shot, shrieking, bursting shells. The sun but a few minutes before so brilliant was now darkened. Through this smoky darkness came the missiles of death, plowing great furrows of destruction among our men, whole columns going down like grass before the scythe. The scene of carnage and death beggars description. Not for the world would the writer look upon such a sight again. In any direction might be seen guns, swords, haversacks, heads, limbs, flesh and bones in confusion or dangling in the air or bounding on the earth. The ground shook as if in the throes of an earthquake. The teamsters, two or more miles away, declared that the sash in the windows of buildings where they were shook and chattered as if shaken by a violent wind. Over us, in front, behind, in our midst, through our ranks and everywhere, came death-dealing missiles. I am reminded by this awful scene, produced by this fearful artillery fire, of the remark made by Colonel Stephen D. Lee, commanding Confederate artillery at Sharpsburg, to one of his artillery officers after the battle: "Sharpsburg was artillery hell." Be this as it may, the artillery fire at Sharpsburg was not comparable to that of the third day at Gettysburg. During all this nearly two hours of horror the men remained steadfast at their posts—excepting those who had not been knocked out of place by shell and shot.

It must not be supposed that men were not alarmed, for doubtless many a poor fellow thought his time had come—and pray? Yes, great big, stout-hearted men prayed, loudly, too, and they were in earnest, for if men ever had need of the care and protection of our Heavenly Father, it was now.

The position was a trying one, indeed; much more so than had we been engaged in close combat, and quite as perilous, for then we should not have felt so much the terrible strain, could we have rendered blow for blow; but it was as if we were placed where we were for target practice for the Union batteries. To the left of my position, and not thirty feet away, eight men were killed or wounded by one shot, while still nearer to me a solid shot trounced a man, lifting him three feet from the earth, killing him but not striking him. Many of the shots causing much damage were from enfilading fire from a Union battery at the Cemetery.

I feel confident in stating that not less than 300 of Pickett's men were killed or injured by artillery fire.

Corporal Jesse B. Young

Near 2:50 P.M., as the artillery fire had practically ceased, there came the order, "Fall in!" and brave General Pickett, coming close by where I lay wounded, called out: "Up, men, and to your posts! Don't forget today that you are from old Virginia!" The effect of this word upon the men was electrical. The regiments were quickly in line, closing to the left over the dead and wounded—the ranks now reduced by the losses occasioned by the shelling to about 4,400 men of the division, and I am satisfied that Kemper's brigade, the smallest of the division, did not then number over 1,250. The advance now began, the men calling out to the wounded and others: "Goodbye, boys! Goodbye!" Unable to move, I could not accompany this advance—did not see, hear, observe or know what thereafter happened only from the statement of others. I will not attempt to state, but for a reasonable and fair report thereof will give the published statement of an intelligent Union soldier (a Massachusetts man) who observed the movement of Pickett's division, which is as follows:

"But what is Gettysburg, either in its first day's Federal defeat, or its second day's terrible slaughter around Little Round Top, without the third day's immortal charge by Pickett and his brave Virginians! * * * Then Pickett and his brave legions stood up and formed for the death struggle: three remnants of brigades, consisting of Garnett's—the 8th, 18th, 19th, 28th and 56th Virginia; Armistead's brigade—the 9th, 14th, 38th, 53d, 57th Virginia; Kemper's brigade—1st, 3d, 7th, 11th, 24th Virginia. Their tattered flags bore the scars of a score of battles, and from their ranks the merciless bullet had already taken two-thirds their number. In compact ranks: their front scarcely covering two of Hancock's brigades, with flags waiving as if for a gala day. * * * It was nearly a mile to the Union lines, and as they advanced over the open plain the Federal artillery opened again, plowing great lanes through their solid ranks, but they closed up to guide center, as if upon dress parade. When half way over, Pickett halted his division amidst a terrible fire of shot and shell, and changed his direction by an oblique movement, coolly and beautifully made. * * * To those who have ever faced artillery fire it is marvellous and unexplainable how human beings could have advanced under the terrific fire of a hundred cannon, every inch of air being laden with the missiles of death; but in splendid formation they still came bravely on till within range of the musketry; then the blue line of Hancock's corps arose and poured into their ranks a murderous fire. With a wild yell the rebels pushed on, unfalteringly, crossed the Federal lines and laid hands upon eleven cannon.

"Men fired into each other's faces; there were bayonet thrusts, cutting with sabres, hand-to-hand contests, oaths, curses, yells and hurrahs. The Second corps fell back behind the guns to allow the use of grape and double cannister, and as it tore through the rebel ranks at only a few paces distant, the dead and wounded were piled in ghastly heaps; still on they came up to the very muzzles of their guns; they were blown away from the cannon's mouth, but yet they did not waiver. Pickett had taken the key to the position, and the glad shout of victory was heard, as, the very impersonation of a soldier, he still forced his troops to the crest of Cemetery Ridge. Kemper and Armistead broke through Hancock's line, scaled the hill and planted their flags on its crest. Just before Armistead was shot, he placed his flag upon a captured cannon and cried: 'Give them the cold steel, boys!' But valor could do no more, the handful of braves had won immortality, but could not conquer an army. * * * Pickett, seeing his supports gone, his Generals Kemper, Armistead and Garnett killed or wounded, every field officer of three brigades gone, three-fourths of his men killed or captured, himself untouched, but broken-hearted, gave the order for retreat, but, band of heroes as they were, they fled not; but amidst that still continuous, terrible fire, they slowly, sullenly, recrossed the plain— all that was left of them, but few of five thousand."

Pickett's division was the only organized body of Confederates that crossed the stone fence. In a letter of General Kemper to me he gives a short description, and but brief, of this wonderful charge, in which he states: "I think General Garnett and myself were the only officers of Pickett's division who went into the battle mounted and remained mounted until shot down. My recollection is that I fell just about the time our men began to give back. I was close enough to the enemy to distinguish features and expressions of faces, and thought I observed and could identify the individual who shot me. Quickly afterwards a Federal officer, with several of his men, took possession of me, placing me on a blanket, started to carry me, as he said, to a Federal surgeon, when some of our men, firing over my body, recaptured me and carried me to our rear.

"As to how the three brigades of our division advanced in line of battle when the artillery ceased firing; as to how the gaps were closed up as men fell and the general alignment was well preserved; as to the cul-de-sac of death, our unsupported, or very badly supported division was hurled into; as to the last unavailing grapple with the overwhelming numbers of the enemy: all these are matters about which you doubtless know as much as I do."

As already stated, it was 1,430 yards from our position to that occupied by the Union infantry; it was practically open field. It was the longest charge in open ground under heavy fire that our troops were ever required to make. Indeed, this was the most remarkable charge made in the annals of warfare.

The Union army, under General Burnside, at the Battle of Fredericksburg against Marye's Hill, made as many as fourteen distinct charges as brave and gallant as were ever made by any soldiers, at some points leaving their dead within a few yards of the Confederate lines, but each time repulsed with heavy loss, but the fact must not be overlooked that these charging columns had fairly good cover to within four hundred yards of the Confederate line.

Had the Confederate assaulting column had a shorter run with protected cover, it is almost certain that the Union lines would have been broken, the Federal army cut in twain, forced to rapid retreat to avoid capture or destruction. Again, it is manifest that had the Federal army been in the open on the third day as on the first and for most part on the second day, General Meade's Union army would have been crushed. As it was, in a well-protected position, and the battle well conducted by General Meade, he barely escaped defeat—too badly crippled to promptly pursue the Confederates.

General Meade was a good soldier, and the Union army of the Potomac made a splendid fight. No doubt General Meade and the Army of the Potomac were proud of their achievement at Gettysburg, for they had been hammered so much and so often by the Army of Northern Virginia that they doubtless expected the same old bill of fare. A little relief was comforting; the other fellows were now sore, for Gettysburg battle was a sad and gloomy one for the Army of Northern Virginia and the Confederacy, but the survivors had not lost their old-time spirit; they soon recuperated, and were themselves again ready for the fray.

In the battles from the Rapidan to the James in the Spring and Summer of 1864, the soldiers of the Army of Northern Virginia showed that they had not lost their old-time spirit, pluck, and fighting qualities, and if the more than twenty thousand men lost by General Lee at Gettysburg had been with him in the Wilderness, in the Spring of 1864, General Grant would not have reached the James by that route. At Gettysburg General Meade had about 105,000 men; General Lee about 62,000. These figures are given by Colonel Taylor, a member of General Lee's staff, and adjutant-general of the army, taken, as he states, from the official records. General Meade himself states his strength not less than 95,000 men. The Federal loss was 23,049; Confederate, 20,451.

The loss in Pickett's division was 2,888; in Kemper's brigade, 58 killed, 356 wounded and 317 captured. In the 7th Virginia regiment the loss was 67. In Company D, David C. Akers, Daniel Bish, Jesse Barrett and John P. Sublett were killed; Lieutenant E. R. Walker and E. M. Stone, Sergeant Taylor and myself, Corporal Young, Privates William C. Fortner, James H. Fortner, J. J. Hurt, John F. Jones (leg amputated), John Meadows, W. W. Muncey and D. L. Sarver, wounded, and John W. Hight captured; total 17—over sixty per cent of the number led into action. By this statement it will be seen that my Company D came out of the Battle of Gettysburg with but 11 men. J. B. Young belonged to the color guard of the 7th regiment. The color bearer, Lieutenant Watson, with his guards, eight sergeants and corporals going into the battle were all either killed or wounded. Our colors fell into the hands of the 82d New York infantry, commanded by Captain John Darrow. Corporal Young was the eighth man who had the colors during the fight, carrying them within a few feet of the enemy's line behind the stone fence, where he was wounded and captured. The colors were then taken by —— Tolbert, a mere boy of ours, who bore them forward to the stone fence, where he intended to plant them, but was shot in the head.

The colors were then grabbed by the man who fired the shot and carried back into the Union lines.

The loss in officers in Pickett's division was something fearful to contemplate. General Garnett was killed, Armistead mortally and Kemper dangerously wounded. Of the whole complement of generals and field officers, aggregating about 48, only one lieutenant-colonel was left. The division was nearly annihilated. General Kemper fell into the enemy's hands in field hospital the second day after he was wounded. So bad was his wound, and he was believed to be so near death, that a coffin was prepared for him, which he refused to use. He survived, and afterwards became Governor of Virginia, serving with distinction and much honor from his countrymen. During his gubernatorial term he carried in his hip a leaden bullet of standard weight and size.

Of the wounded in Company D, Lieutenant Stone, Corporal Young, Privates William C. Fortner, James H. Fortner, Jones, Hurt and the writer fell into the hands of the enemy; Stone, Young, William C. Fortner, Jones and Hurt on the field; James H. Fortner and the writer the second day thereafter in the field hospital. Several of the men of Company D in the charge went over the stone wall, only a few getting back, among them Sergeant Taylor, and he wounded. Thomas N. Mustain, a valiant soldier, transferred from Company D to the 57th Virginia regiment, went over the stone wall, and while lying under the captured Union batteries was severely wounded in the neck.

Company E of the 7th regiment had four men—Alec Legg, John Canady, Willis Welch and Joseph Welch—killed during the artillery duel by the explosion of a shell. The company carried into the charge but one officer, Lieutenant Stone, and seventeen men, all of whom except one man were killed, wounded or captured.

Recurring to the wounding of myself at the closing of the artillery duel, I was at my post on the left of the regiment, which threw me under the shade of a friendly apple tree which chanced to stand there. I lay down near Colonel Mayo, of the 3d regiment, and Colonel Patton of the 7th, near the feet of the latter. A little before the artillery fire ceased, a Union battery at the Cemetery on our left front had on us an enfilading fire with accurate range, which threw shell and solid shot into our ranks. A shell from this battery struck the heads of two men of the 3d regiment, taking them off above the ears, exploding almost on me, not only killing the two men and wounding me, but also wounding Lieutenant Brown of the 7th regiment, and another, who lay close on my right. Just a moment before this shell came, I had raised my head up to get, if possible, a breath of fresh air, whereupon Lieutenant Brown said to me: "You had better put your head down or you may get it knocked off." I replied: "A man had about as well die that way as to suffocate for want of air." The words had scarcely escaped my lips when the shell exploded, which for a few moments deprived me of my breath and sensibility; I found myself lying off from the position I was in when struck, gasping for breath. My ribs on left side were broken, some fractured, left lung badly contused, and left limbs and side paralyzed. My Colonel Patton, sprang to his feet inquiring if I was badly hurt. I asked for water, the first thing a wounded man wants, and the Colonel had it brought to me. The marvel is that I escaped the explosion of that shell without being torn to shreds. Harry Snidow and another of my old company brought a blanket, placing it at the base of the apple tree, where they set me up against the tree. Just then the order came for the men to fall in for the charge, which has already been described. Colonel Mayo, after the war, describing this day's battle and the part taken by our division, refers to me as "one left for dead under that apple tree." I still live, while the brave and good Colonel has passed to the Great Beyond.

In a few minutes after the men moved forward, the "litter bearers" picked me up and bore me back into the woods to our field hospital, where our surgeons, Drs. Oliver and Worthington, did for me all in their power. About dark I was removed by ambulance to the shed of a farmer's barn, a mile or more away, on Willoughby Run, to the place where General Kemper had been removed, the farmer placing him in his dwelling house. I visited this same house twenty-two years later, where I saw distinctly the stains of General Kemper's blood on the floor. The shed in which I was placed was filled with the wounded and dying. Throughout that long night and until a little before dawn, I spoke to no one, and no one to me, never closed my eyes in sleep; the surgeons close by being engaged in removing the limbs of those necessary to be amputated, and all night long I heard nothing but the cries of the wounded and the groans of the dying, the agonies of General Kemper, who lay near by, being frequently heard. Everything in the barn was dark, but near dawn I discovered a flickering light advancing toward me: it was borne by John W. Grubb, of our regiment, who had been sent by our surgeon to look after me. Comrade Grubb was very kind to me, preparing for me a day or two later a bed and shelter in the orchard, to which I was removed, but he was taken away a prisoner by the Federals.

During the morning of Sunday many of our wounded men were brought in, among them Captain John H. Parr, adjutant of the 7th regiment, and Lieutenant Lewis Bane of the 24th regiment. Some of these wounded men died during the day.

During Sunday night and the following day the Confederate army was withdrawing from the field. Our brigade surgeon, Dr. Morton, and General

Early made visits to the field hospital, urging all the men able to ride in wagons to go, of which a goodly number availed themselves. Shortly after the Confederate rear guard had passed the field hospital where I was, the Federal advance guard appeared, the Federal surgeons taking charge of us.

Lee's army continued the retreat into Virginia, and I did not join my command for service for four months after, at Taylorsville.

CHAPTER XIX

- Sketches and Incidents While a Wounded Prisoner.

- How Long in the Field Hospital.

- The Walk to Gettysburg and Kindness Shown Me by a Federal Captain.

- In Box Cars and Ride to Baltimore.

- What Occurred in Baltimore.

- To Chester, Pa.

- Dr. Schafer and Another.

- Paroled and Back to Dixie.

The Federal surgeon who took charge of us in the field hospital at Gettysburg made an examination of my wound and gave instructions that I should receive no solid food, but be fed lemonade and spirits. Up to this time and for days subsequent I wanted no food, having no desire for it. A Union soldier from Ohio was my nurse, who treated me with kindness. This soldier would get the daily Philadelphia newspapers and read to me the war news. Among other things, that Lee's army, badly broken, was making rapid retreat for Virginia; that the loyal Potomac was at high tide, could not be crossed; that General Meade's army was pushing the Confederates, would soon be up with them; then the following day he read that Lee's army was around Williamsport, could not get away; that Meade's army was now up and preparing for attack, only waiting the arrival of food supplies and ammunition. When receiving these papers and reading to me, the soldier's face was all aglow with joyous expression, to which he gave voice by saying: "The rebels will all be captured and that will end the war." To this I could only smile inwardly. July 13 my nurse, with his paper and a smile, came to read me the news. I was prepared for the worst—but when he read, it was that General Meade was now up, fully ready, and the attack would be made tomorrow, when Lee and his army would be captured, or driven into the river. Morning came, and the nurse and his paper, but as he approached I noted quite a change in his expression; he read, when General Meade moved out to attack the rebel army, behold! "the old fox had gone," having crossed the river the night before!

July 20 we were ordered to be removed from the field hospital, but to what place we did not know. A Union captain of Pennsylvania, with a squad of soldiers, conducted us to the railway station at Gettysburg nearly a mile away. I should not have gone, as the journey came near finishing me up. The captain was exceedingly kind, affording me all the help in his power. The whole of the wounded squad was put aboard box cars at night, landing in Baltimore at dawn, I more dead than alive. I felt sure, as the rough train rolled along, that I was near death. John H. Peck, of the 24th Virginia, who had a wound in the head, was with us, and by encouragement and otherwise rendered me much assistance.

In Baltimore the cars were run up far into the city, where we left the train, being immediately surrounded by a cordon of soldiers and police, with a number of ladies, men and boys, who endeavored to supply us with food, but were beaten off by the guards, who quickly landed us inside the high plank fence surrounding the grounds of West Building Hospital. The ladies again renewed their efforts to supply us with food by tossing it over the high fence, but were repulsed by the soldiers' bayonets—which we still think was a mean act. With James H. Fortner, of my company, who had a severe flesh wound in the thigh, I lay down beside the fence in the shade, unable to move further. In an hour or less an order came to get into ranks. Neither Fortner nor myself moved, being determined to remain and take chances. Fortunate for us that we remained, for the poor fellows who marched away landed in Point Lookout prison; the men seriously wounded, however, being sent to hospital at Chester, Pennsylvania, I among the number, with Fortner. I had requested Fortner to remain with me, for should I die he could inform my people. After comrades had marched away, Fortner and I dragged ourselves into the hospital building, lying down on the bare floor.

During the evening two ladies came in where we were, one of whom inquired: "Where are you from?" "Virginia," I answered. "Then you are not more than half rebels." Replying, I said: "Well, I am a full-blooded rebel, whatever the people of Virginia may be." From their constant glances at each other and toward the door, and from the expressions on their faces, I was well satisfied that at heart they were true Southern spirits, angels of mercy, and had used the above language to us fearing the walls had ears. Presently one inquired if we wanted anything to eat, and being told we would be glad to have milk, they furnished it and departed.

That night we were placed on cots near each other, in a clean, airy room. Fortner, in endeavoring to assist me to rise, fell on his wounded leg, which caused him great pain. The second night thereafter, we were placed in box cars, passing next day through Wilmington, Delaware, where a curious, motley crowd gathered to see us; they peeped and peered at us as if astonished that we did not have hoofs and horns. That evening we reached Chester, on the Delaware, where we were placed in hospital (now Crozer

Theological Seminary). Here we met a number of the men we had parted from in Baltimore, among them John H. Peck and J. B. Young, the latter of Company D. The surgeon of our ward was Dr. Schafer of Philadelphia, who was kind to us. He, however, soon went away, being succeeded by a doctor from Franklin County—a Virginia renegade, who was insulting, mean and cowardly, and the wounded gave him many a hard thrust.

While in this hospital several ladies and gentlemen from the State of Connecticut came into the ward, engaging me in conversation about the war, saying among other things that the South in seceding was wrong and unjustifiable, that the proper course, or that which should have been pursued, was to fight in the Union. To which I replied that they were in some respects much like many of the Northern people who encouraged the South to take action, that they would be with us, but when the test came were found on the other side. Again, that I could not see well how we could remain in the Union and at the same time try to strangle and destroy the government of which we claimed to be a part; that it was certain, had we done so and been overthrown, we would have been traitors sure enough and most likely have gone to the gibbet.

After a stay at Chester of thirty days or less, all who desired to go South were paroled, I among the number, and were transported by boat to City Point, thence by rail to Richmond. The authorities ordered us to Camp Lee, a Confederate recruiting station near the city. This we did not like, and a few of us determined to go home, or to our commands, and we made the start, but were halted a little way out of the city by some local troops, who charged us with an effort to desert. We explained the situation, but this did not satisfy them. I met with a Confederate enrolling officer, who kindly took me home with him, giving me written pass to my command, then in camp on the Rapidan, whither I went, and was quite a surprise to Drs. Morton and Worthington and my comrades, who told me that they supposed me dead. Dr. Morton, who was wearing a soft felt black hat, said to me: "When I left you in the field hospital at Gettysburg I never expected to see you again in life. You were as black in the face as this hat." I soon had furlough and went home, where I remained until the first of November, when I learned I had been exchanged, and at once left to rejoin my command.

I forgot to relate an incident worthy of mention, at least to me. In the hospital at Chester, when Dr. Schafer already referred to examined me, he said: "Young man, do you know you are nearly dead?" I gasped for breath, saying: "I think it quite possible." Placing a small bottle of something within my reach, he charged me to take of this when inclined to cough, without waiting until the coughing began, for he said: "If you have a spell of coughing you would surely die of hemorrhage in ten minutes." He then procured for me a nurse, an Irishman, the father of two sons in the Union army, who had been in the Battle of Shiloh, Tenn. In speaking fondly of these boys he wept like a child. Fortunate it was that I fell into the hands of this kindly-hearted man, for a mother could not have cared more tenderly for her son than he did for me. Such cases confirm the fact that human sympathy asserts itself even in the rancors of war.

CHAPTER XX

I joined my command, then at Taylorsville, Virginia, whither it had been sent to rendezvous and recruit, at the same time guarding the bridges over the North and South Anna rivers. Our long stay at Taylorsville during the months of November and December, 1863, and for part of January, 1864, gave ample opportunity to discuss the serious aspect of affairs. We had received a stunning blow at Gettysburg, evidenced by the absence forever of brave men whose places could not be supplied. Naturally the query was often made, how long will the war last? When will it end? What are our prospects for success? Will it continue until the last man falls? What do the Northern people mean? Is it their intention to subjugate the states, and overthrow the citadel of liberty itself? They call us rebels—can a sovereign be a rebel? We had been taught that the states were sovereign and that their governments were instituted to secure certain inalienable rights, with which their Creator had endowed them—among these, life, liberty and the pursuit of happiness, and that the security of all these resided with the states and the people thereof, and not with their Federal agent. These and many other matters were discussed, and the general conclusion arrived at was: we will have to fight it out.

In the last days of November, the Federal army, under General Meade, crossed the Rapidan, making a feint as if to attack the Army of Northern Virginia, but instead re-crossed the river, seeming to have crossed for no other purpose than to cross back again. We had orders to be ready to go to General Lee's aid.

While at Taylorsville the Rev. Dr. Blackwell, who had resided in the cities of Norfolk and Portsmouth, Virginia, during General Butler's reign of terror therein, delivered to our brigade a lecture on Butler, his troops, and the noble women of those cities. After describing the insults of the Federal soldiery, and the sacrifices and heroic conduct of the women, he pronounced upon them an eulogy, a part only of which is recalled, and is now here reproduced; he began by saying:

"Woman is lovely, but not a goddess. We call her angel, but she has no wings to soar quite beyond the bounds of terrene. She is the loveliest form of beauty known to earth, and presents the purest type of that sweet companionship that awaits us in the bright land of the hereafter; but still she is flesh and blood, loves to steal from the bowers of her paradise and dwell with men, mingle in the common concerns and partake of the common infirmities of the human race. As the graceful vine entwines itself around the sturdy oak when riven by the lightnings of Heaven, so she, though the feebler, gentler sex, is the prop upon which the sterner sex in the midst of revolution often leans for repose. * * * And when the history of this revolution is fully written, these noble women will stand in the front ranks of that illustrious galaxy of Southern females whose heroic acts and beauteous deeds have illuminated our Heavens, and thrown a halo of fadeless glory around the noble women of Norfolk and Portsmouth."

Our General Pickett was married, as I now recall, in September, 1863, in Petersburg, Virginia, to Miss Corbell, a lovely, highly cultivated Virginia woman who occasionally rode with the General through our camps, attending the division review. Later, when Baby George arrived, he was exhibited in the camps, the soldiers eagerly fondling him; nor was his linen as spotless or his humor as sweet when handed back to his mother or nurse as when the boys received him.

The General and boy have both passed to the Great Beyond, but the lovely wife and mother still lives to brighten the memories of husband and son, the noble dead of the division, and to cheer the hearts of the brave men who counted it the honor of their lives to have marched with the noble Pickett, made famous for all time to come by his charge at Gettysburg, now celebrated in song and literature.

Our rations were not abundant while at Taylorsville; one pint of unsieved meal and a quarter of a pound of bacon per day. Coffee was made of parched wheat rye, and sometimes of rice when we had it. Occasionally the men managed to get turnips or potatoes, of which they made fairly good soup. There was so little of the bacon that we could not afford to fry it, so we generally ate it raw, with an ash or Johnny cake; we had but few cooking utensils, and had need of few.

Religious services were held when possible; the weather for the most part was too inclement to have open air services, and we had no church. Such services as were had were generally in the messes, or conducted in the quarters of J. Tyler Frazier, to which all were invited.

Being under orders to march, our preparations therefor completed, we took up the movement January 20, going through Richmond and Petersburg, where we were put aboard cars and transported to Goldsboro, N.C., remaining there a few days. Leaving camp at Goldsboro January 29, we proceeded to Kinston, on the Neuse River, thence through the swamps and bogs, crossing the Trent River to the vicinity of Newbern, N.C., where we made some captures of prisoners and stores, and blew up a Federal gunboat lying in the river, under the forts, which was accomplished by Colonel Wood, with his marines. A section of 3d New York artillery—two guns—was captured, together with several hundred prisoners, among them 35 or more of the 2d Loyal North Carolina regiment, who had been soldiers in our army, deserted, and joined the enemy. These men were recognized and sent back under guard to Kinston.

Our people found Newbern better prepared for defense than was anticipated, and after some strong reconnaissances on all the roads, gathering up all the supplies within reach that could be transported, at dark, February 3, we silently folded our tents and stole away, floundering all night along through the swamps and mud, crossing the Trent a little after dawn. During the night we passed through extensive turpentine orchards, which the men set fire to, and by the light of which many sloughs were avoided. Our movement continued until Kinston was reached, where we rested a few days.

The next day after reaching Kinston the court-martial was convened for the trial of the thirty-five deserters referred to, who had been captured wearing

United States uniforms and with guns in their hands, fighting under the flag of the enemy. The guilt of twenty-two of them being fully established, they were sentenced to be hanged; the sentence being approved by the department commander, was carried into execution a few days thereafter in the vicinity of our camp: a gruesome piece of business, which duty did not require me to witness.

About the middle of February we moved on westward to Goldsboro. Rations were still short, and there was some complaint by the farmers of the loss of hogs. This complaint was not without foundation, for fresh pork was found in some of the camps, and the offenders punished, a penalty, as the writer believes, not deserved. Most of these charges were made against the 24th Virginia regiment, one against some of the teamsters of our regiment. A member of Company D was charged with being the informant, though he helped eat the hog, but whether the charge was true or false, the informant made the disclosure in order to get a furlough, which he received, but never came back—deserted. This same informant had been wounded at the second battle of Manassas, and on his return to the command at Goldsboro claimed that he was not able for service, taking up lodgings with some of the teamsters. He wrote a letter to General Lee, which ran about as follows:

"Dear General: I am a member of Company D, 7th Virginia Infantry. I was wounded at the second battle of Manassas and am unfit for duty in the field. I am a pretty fair shoemaker, and if I can be detailed, I am willing to render all the services I can."

General Lee transmitted the letter to the regiment and the men had a good deal of fun out of ———. Soon after he became informant as to hog stealing, got the furlough, and deserted, as above stated—good riddance to bad rubbish.

A member of Company B, 7th regiment, who was under death sentence for desertion, was kept under strict guard with ball and chain. Late one evening an order came for his execution the next day. I carried the order to the officer of the guard, whose instructions were to double the guard and see that their guns were loaded. The condemned man's brother was a member of the guard, who, on ascertaining that his brother was to be shot the next day, requested that I send Rev. J. Tyler Frazier to see him. Frazier happened to be out of the camp; as soon as he returned, I accompanied him to see the man, but he refused to listen to Mr. Frazier; in fact, the man did not believe he would be shot until the next morning when the wagon drove up with his coffin and he was required to ride thereon to the place of execution, where he died from the fire of a platoon of men of his own command.

March 5 we moved by rail to Wilmington, thence by steamer to Smithfield, near the mouth of the Cape Fear River. The 24th regiment was sent to garrison Forts Caswell and Campbell, while we remained in camp near Smithfield.

I find in a letter written by me from Smithfield, March 14, the following: "It has been nine days since our brigade arrived at this place. One regiment, the 24th, has been sent to garrison Forts Caswell and Campbell. I have just returned from a visit to the former. We crossed over in an open boat, the distance being two miles. There was quite a lively time at the forts this morning, when the blockade runner 'Lucy,' in attempting to run in, was beached, the enemy making attempt to capture her, but he was driven off by our batteries."

Lieut. Thomas S. Taylor

Here oysters were cheap and readily procured, the men cooking them in various ways. Some roasted them in the shell, some ate them raw, and some mixed them in corn dough and baked them. We did not like the coast and longed for our Virginia hills. Under orders we left Smithfield aboard a steamer for Wilmington. The river was full of torpedoes and we were in dread of being blown up. The situation was in some measure relieved by Bill Dean and his Glee Club, who sang: "Oh! Carry Me Back to Old Virginia Once More."

Wilmington was reached Saturday, the 26th, where the ground was covered with a light snow, which increased in depth as we receded from the coast. We moved by rail from Wilmington to Goldsboro, where we went into camp until Friday, the first of April, when the march was again taken up through snow and mud to Tarboro, thence through Greenville, crossing over to the waters of the Roanoke, to the vicinity of Plymouth, N.C., where on the 18th a portion of Hoke's brigade (21st Georgia regiment), assailed late in the evening an outlying fort, in which assault Colonel Mercer was killed and the assault repulsed. Later the same evening this fort was surrounded by a portion of our brigade with a cloud of sharpshooters and artillery, which prevented the garrison from handling their guns, and the fort finally surrendered. The investing force of the town were the brigades of Ransom, Hoke and Terry, formerly Kemper's.

Sergeant William Parrott of Charlottesville and I that night bore a flag of truce to the enemy's lines, under which demand for the surrender of the town was made, but refused. During the night the Confederate iron clad ram "Albemarle" came down the Roanoke River and aided in the assault next morning, when the enemy's works and the town were carried, the garrison surrendering when all hope of successful resistance was gone. Our brigade was moved across the Washington road, whereon the enemy was attempting to escape. In this movement we were brought under the fire of the heavy guns in the forts, which at close range gave us a severe shelling, whereby quite a number of men of the brigade were injured—a few in our regiment—but two in Company D—A. L. Fry and John W. East—slightly wounded. Soon after occupying the road referred to and close up to the enemy's entrenchments, there came at a headlong run up to our line, and before he discovered us, a big, black, burly negro soldier, the first of his kind we had seen. The negro was so badly frightened that had it been possible he would have changed his color.

The fruits of this victory, at comparatively small cost, were the Federal commander, General Wessels, and 1,600 prisoners, besides about 700 negroes, 2,000 small arms, and valuable quartermaster and commissary stores, the capture and sinking of one or more Federal gunboats. From the commissary and sutler's stores the men obtained bountiful supplies of food, underwear, boots and shoes. The Federal loss in this battle, other than prisoners, artillery and stores already mentioned, was 41 killed and 59 wounded. The Confederate loss, 124 killed and 174 wounded. Our enjoyment was but brief, however, for that evening we took the road to Washington, a town at the head of Pamlico Sound, marching rapidly, so that by night we were in the neighborhood of our destination, which early next morning General Hoke was preparing to invest, when it was discovered that the enemy had evacuated it; disgracing themselves and their flag before their departure by arson and pillage.

General Hoke, determined to push his successes, marched immediately upon Newbern, demanding its surrender, which, being refused, he was preparing to carry by assault, when he was directed to hasten to the relief of Petersburg, now threatened by a strong Federal army under General Butler.

At Tarboro, B. L. Hoge was taken sick and sent to hospital, and J. B. Croy had been sent on detached service to the Blackwater region. How many of Company D were on this expedition to Plymouth, Washington and Newbern, I am unable to state, but I know the company had been much reduced in numbers. Lieutenant Stone was still a prisoner at Fort Delaware, Lieutenant Walker, disabled at Gettysburg, had been retired; Captain Bane and Lieutenant Mullins were the only commissioned officers with us.

In May, 1864, the Federal General Butler landed at City Point, on the James, with an army of more than 25,000 men, and feeling his way carefully and slowly toward Petersburg, had on the 9th reached Swift Creek, three miles north of the city. Confronting him was General Pickett, with a small number of Carolina troops, and a few pieces of artillery. Pickett kept his men so well in hand and so maneuvered as to conceal from his adversary his real weakness. In this situation and while the Confederates were far away, near Newbern, with the Federals threatening Richmond and Petersburg, General Hoke, in front of Newbern, received an order to repair with haste to Petersburg. About dark on May 6 we left the front of Newbern, the head of the column directed for Petersburg, about 175 miles away. The 1st Virginia had hastened through to Kinston, where it obtained railroad transportation, which carried it to Jarrett's, twenty miles south of Petersburg. Our column, taking a bee line, moved night and day, having to halt occasionally at the tidewater streams to build bridges out of round logs thrown into the water and fastened together with grapevines. Reaching Stony Creek, twenty miles or more south of Petersburg, we found the railroad bridge destroyed by the Federal cavalry. The situation at Petersburg was so pressing as to demand the presence of the troops without delay. All the rolling stock of every kind of the railroad at that point was rushed to meet us, and we boarded the cars just wherever we met them. By 11 o'clock Thursday, May 12, we were in the city, and General Butler had lost his opportunity. Never before had we done such marching. Mr. D. H. Hill, in his Confederate Military History of North Carolina, page 248, speaking of this march of General Hoke from Newbern to Petersburg, says: "This march of General Hoke's troops stands at West Point as the most rapid movement of troops on record."

Apparently the whole populace, men, women and children, of Petersburg had gathered to welcome us, their deliverers from the presence and hand of General Butler, whose notoriety in New Orleans, Norfolk and Portsmouth had won for him the appellation "Beast Butler," a reputation world-wide. General Butler was, therefore, regarded by these people as a menace to the safety of property and helpless women and children. This is why everybody in Petersburg shouted for joy when we entered the city and marched across the Appomattox to interpose between them and Butler's troops. We went forward to Swift Creek, taking position on the east side of the turnpike road in front of the enemy's skirmishers. The shades of night now having fallen, we lay on our arms, discovering next morning by the advance of our skirmishers that the enemy had withdrawn from our front, whereupon we proceeded along the road leading to Richmond, the rear guard being fired upon as we passed the "Halfway House." Reaching the outer defenses of Dreury's Bluff, our brigade, now commanded by Brigadier-General W. R. Terry, was placed in battle line on the west side of the aforesaid turnpike road, facing south—having by the day's march placed ourselves between the enemy and Richmond.

CHAPTER XXI

- **Battle of Dreury's Bluff.**

- **The Forces Engaged.**

- **Casualties.**

- **The Pursuit of General Butler's Troops.**

- **Bombardment at Howlett's House.**

- **The Wounding of Lieutenant John W. Mullins.**

- **His Death.**

- **Withdrawal from Howlett's House.**

General Beauregard, in command of the department, arrived on the morning of the 14th, having passed with a cavalry escort entirely around the enemy's left. About noon of the 15th we were moved to an inner line of defenses, which shortened the line to be defended; thus was made necessary by the smallness of our force, for it appears that the Confederates had only 13,000 men with which to meet Butler's 40,000. This Confederate force was divided, two or three brigades remaining at Petersburg under General Whiting. No help could be had from the Army of Northern Virginia, then engaged in desperate struggle at Spottsylvania, with the Federal Army of the Potomac.

It was made known to us on the evening of the 15th that at a council of war held by General Beauregard and his subordinates it had been determined to attack General Butler's army next morning at daylight, and that the division of General Ransom, to which our brigade (Terry's) belonged, was to lead the attack. Late in the day, Sunday, we marched toward the James River to a point overlooking Kingsland Creek, behind which, on the higher ground beyond, the enemy was in line of battle in force, sheltered by temporary log breastworks, a small body of Confederate cavalry guarding the Confederate left. Being supplied with sixty rounds of cartridges, we lay down in a skirt of timber near the old stage road leading from Richmond to Petersburg, a little more than three-fourths of a mile from the enemy's line. We were informed that we should be up at 2 A.M., march forward and open the battle at daylight. Some who had passed unscathed through the ordeal of a dozen battles were to go down in this, among them the gallant boy Walker, of the 11th regiment, who had borne aloft and planted on the enemy's works at Gettysburg the flag of this regiment, having his horse killed under him there and a number of bullets through his clothing.

To fight this battle of Dreury's Bluff was imperative, and to become the assailants was a necessity, for if the enemy should maintain his position then occupied in front of Dreury's Bluff (only seven miles below Richmond) and General Grant continued his flank movement to the James River until he formed a junction with General Butler, the fate of Richmond, and most probably of the Confederacy, would have been decided a year earlier; hence this battle, and the necessity of fighting it successfully, which we did.

During the early part of the night preceding, I visited the artillery company of Captain David A. French, from my county. Captain French was absent that evening, the company under the command of his brave Lieutenant D. W. Mason. Captain French arrived next day during the progress of the battle. Lieutenant Mason led his company in the thickest of the fight, sustaining his already brilliant record as a brave soldier. Promptly at 2 A.M. on Monday, the 16th, we were roused from our slumbers and quickly gotten into line, discarding all baggage—indeed, everything that would make a noise calculated to arouse the enemy. Stealing quietly out of the woods, we proceeded down the old stage road, through a field, across Kingsland Creek, where we halted, forming a line of battle. The Alabama brigade of General Gracie, and the North Carolina brigade of General Hoke, formed the front line, with Generals Terry's and Fry's commands four hundred yards in rear, forming the second line. The assaulting force could not have numbered four thousand men all told. What was in front of us we did not know, being already enveloped by a dense fog. The columns now formed, the brigade of Gracie led off, ours following at close distance. The Federal skirmishers in their rifle pits, alarmed by the commands of our officers, fired rapidly, but at random, as they could not see us on account of the fog; but their fire aroused their main line of battle. The ground over which the attacking column passed was a gradual ascent from the creek bottom for a distance of three hundred yards to the summit, then a slight descent for the same distance to the enemy's battle line, the right of which rested on a swamp rendered almost impenetrable on account of the water, thorns and brambles.

Terry's brigade, only forty or fifty yards in rear of Gracie's, reached the summit almost as soon as Gracie's men, who, as well as ourselves, became immediately exposed to the enemy's fire, which as yet was not effective, for they could not see us, and now as the fire had opened, the smoke therefrom, together with the dense fog, created a darkness in which a man could not be seen a few yards away. General Terry had halted his brigade on the summit, where it was receiving the enemy's fire, now becoming more accurate, causing some of the companies on the right to lie down. Colonel Flowerree, now commanding the 7th Virginia, observing this, called out: "Stand up, men! Don't you see the balls are striking the ground at your feet, and there is greater danger lying down than standing up."

On our immediate right was Barton's brigade, commanded by Colonel Fry. A part of Gracie's men had gotten close to the enemy's line, meeting such stubborn resistance that they lay down and our brigade was ordered forward. Now was the supreme moment. Such a deafening rebel yell! It must have given every Yankee in the region roundabout a cold chill, for to this day they say that hideous rebel yell was dreaded more than bullets. Here on this summit we had stood in awful suspense for twenty minutes or more, exposed to the enemy's fire. It was therefore a positive relief to hear the word: "Forward!" And forward we went, through fog, smoke and leaden hail. At each volley delivered by the enemy, down went numbers of our men, and as yet not a man in our brigade had fired a shot, anxious at least to see something to shoot at, and to get to closer quarters.

The 7th Virginia held the left of the brigade line, overlapping by three or more companies the left of Gracie's line. These companies in the headlong rush saw nothing of Gracie's men, who had halted and laid down. Now near the enemy's firing line, unable to get forward on account of the swamp referred to, Captain Parr, Adjutant, took these three companies by a double quick to a position on the right wing, but before this could be accomplished the regiment had broken the enemy's line—that of a New Jersey regiment of Heckman's brigade—and crossed his breastworks, making a right wheel, uniting with the companies led by Captain Parr, and struck the flank of the 27th Massachusetts regiment, capturing its Colonel (Lee), together with its colors, a large number of prisoners, including General Heckman, the brigade commander, who was captured by Sergeant Blakey of F Company, who surrendered his sword to Colonel Flowerree of our regiment. This incident was witnessed by the writer. This wheel and attack upon the enemy's flank and rear had relieved the pressure on the 1st, 11th and 24th regiments, which for some minutes before were engaged in a hand-to-hand contest with the enemy behind their breastworks; indeed, so close had they gotten that the men did not take time to return ramrods to their thimbles, but ran down the cartridges, fired away, filling the logs of the breastworks and trees with the ramrods. This may be thought a fish story, but it is absolutely true. French's Giles County battery of four guns already mentioned was on the field just to our right and in the hottest of the battle, suffering loss in making a brave fight.

The loss in the 1st, 11th and 24th regiments of our brigade had been severe in officers and men—some companies losing nearly half their number in killed and wounded. The color sergeant of the 11th regiment had a bayonet fixed to the point of his color staff, which he used with effect upon the enemy at the breastworks. The brigade continued its flank movement along the rear of the enemy's position until it had cleared the whole of its original front, and had gained a position looking back towards Kingsland Creek, where it halted and faced about, taking possession of the enemy's log breastworks and fronting the enemy. A short lull now followed, during which an Irish Sergeant of the 1st regiment came to me talking with J. Tyler Frazier, and presented me with a fine black felt hat, lost by some Federal officer in his hurry to get away, about which hat the sequel will appear later. In a few minutes the enemy on our right flank was upon us, and before action could be taken to meet them, fired a volley enfilading our line, but thanks to their bad aim and the fact that the men were mostly lying down, nobody was hurt; however, in making left wheel to meet this assault, four men were injured; among them I recall Sergeant Carpenter of Company A, a gallant soldier, was killed; Sergeant Fry of D Company in the melee fell— he may have stumped his toe. The Confederate troops on our right struck the flank of the enemy, who had flanked us, and repulsed their attack, and with this the battle virtually ended. Butler was retreating and getting away— a thing he was good at. He had had enough and was willing to quit. He retired behind his intrenched line at Bermuda Hundred, where the Confederates "bottled him up."

The Federal casualties in this battle were 422 killed, 2380 wounded, of which 1388 were made prisoners, together with five stand of colors, of which four of the colors and 400 of the prisoners were taken by our brigade, and five field guns were captured. The Confederate casualties were 514 killed, 1086 wounded. In Terry's brigade the losses were as follows:

1st Virginia	12 killed,	25 wounded
7th Virginia	2 killed,	37 wounded
11th Virginia	15 killed,	94 wounded
24th Virginia	28 killed,	108 wounded
	57 killed,	264 wounded
Total		321

The brave Colonel Maury and Major Hambrick of the 24th were wounded, the former severely when within a few feet of the enemy's line, the latter mortally. Company D of the 7th regiment lost John W. East, and John S. Dudley, slightly wounded. The losses in the 7th regiment were less on account of its being less exposed in its flank movement on the enemy's right and rear.

The Confederate troops remained on the battle field that night, burying the dead and caring for the wounded. Early next morning we started in pursuit of the enemy, whom we followed on this and the next day to the Howlett house on the James, where the Confederates had some unfinished earthworks. Reaching the edge of an open field on which the earthworks were located, I was directed to go forward to the works to see what or who was there, and finding the trenches entirely abandoned, I waived my cap, when the 1st and 7th regiments speedily came up and took possession. Here they suffered eleven hours from an unmerciful shelling from a number of Federal gunboats in the river. Several men of the two regiments were killed or injured. Lieutenant John W. Mullins of Company D, in command of the skirmish line, was dangerously wounded in the breast, dying on the 22d of June following. He was a bright and brave young man. Major Howard and Sergeant Tom Fox of the regiment were badly hurt. Withdrawing the evening of the 19th, we went into camp a short distance from the Clay house.

CHAPTER XXII

- **To Richmond.**

- **Captured Flags.**

- **Affair at Milford.**

- **Hanover Junction.**

- **North Anna.**

- **Cold Harbor.**

- **Tom Yowell's Yarn.**

- **John A. Hale and His Prisoner.**

- **Malvern Hill.**

May 20 the brigade marched into Richmond, each of the regiments bearing one of the captured flags taken in the engagement of Dreury's Bluff. In the evening a portion of the command was placed on flat cars and transported to Milford station, on the R.F. and P. railroad, a few miles south of Fredericksburg, where on the next morning we were attacked by the advance of General Grant's army, Torbett's cavalry. The portion of our brigade present now numbered less than 500 men, commanded by Major George F. Norton of the 1st regiment, with Sergeant Major J. R. Pollock acting Assistant Adjutant General. After a spirited contest of more than an hour, in which the repeated charges of the Federal cavalry were repulsed, Major Norton ordered the men to retire, and they withdrew across the river, the Mattapony, Captain Parr and I dismantling the bridge by throwing the planks from the center into the river, thus preventing immediate pursuit by the Federal cavalry. The tough resistance given the Federal advance, together with the story of Tom Yowell of the 7th regiment, given below, caused the Federal General Hancock to halt his command, throw up intrenchments and prepare for an attack. This halt gave General Lee time to reach Hanover Junction in advance of the enemy.

A correspondent of a Northern newspaper with the Union army reported on May 22, "The army under Hancock arrived at Milford yesterday and met a force of the enemy said to be 13,000 strong, drove them through the town and pursued them some distance." The only Confederate troops Hancock met were the 500 above mentioned, and there were no others within several miles.

Tom Yowell had been captured on the skirmish line and was taken to General Hancock, who inquired to what command he belonged. Yowell with much bravado told him we had given Butler the devil a few days before, and that our brigade was the advance of General Lee's army from Spottsylvania, and pointing south to a large white house a mile or more away, said, "That is General Lee's headquarters." Yowell told his story with so much apparent frankness that General Hancock believed it. The Confederate loss in this affair was 70 men, mostly of the 11th regiment, captured, some of whom were wounded. These were cut off from the bridge by the rapid advance of the enemy, some of whom, with those who were cut off, escaped by swimming the river.

Our force joined the main army en route from Spottsylvania to Hanover Junction. Here we were also joined by a portion of Breckenridge's small division from the valley, where a little more than a week before it had defeated the Federal army under General Sigel. On this rapid march from Milford to Hanover Junction, John A. Hale of Company D was unable to keep up and to prevent capture took to the woods, following the line of march, keeping the general direction. Going to a private house for food, he found a Union soldier there on the same errand, whom he captured and brought into our lines.

Held in reserve, we had little or nothing to do with the fighting at the North Anna. On May 27 we made an all day march in the rain, going into camp near Atlee's station. In the evening of the following day a march was made twelve miles in the direction of Hanovertown, camping three miles north of Mechanicsville, following General Grant around the circle. On the evening of the 30th we reached our position in battle line near Cold Harbor, being assigned a place on the left of Law's Alabama brigade and Hoke's division.

At 4 o'clock, June 2, the battle of Cold Harbor began on our right, raging furiously until sunset. By means of an improvised telegraphy, information was received that the enemy had been repulsed. This improvised telegraphy was nothing more than passing word from man to man and on this occasion came, "Pass it along the lines that we have whipped the enemy on the right." Early on the morning of the 3d the battle of Cold Harbor was resumed, Hoke's, Breckenridge's and part of Anderson's divisions being engaged on the right. When the battle ended, we were informed by the same telegraphic line that the enemy had been defeated. On our front had been nothing more than artillery fire, with severe skirmishing. However, as the battle progressed, our division was ordered to be ready to attack the enemy in front, and we were very well satisfied when the order was revoked.

In Breckenridge's division, heavily engaged on the 3d, I had a schoolmate, Lieutenant James K. Peck, of whom I was fond, and for whose safety I was anxious. I was greatly distressed on learning a few days afterwards that he was killed on the 3d.

The Federal casualties in the battle at Cold Harbor were over 10,000; the Confederate 1500. I find no report of casualties in our division, brigade or regiment; no casualties in Company D.

I had the opportunity to look at a portion of the battlefield in front of the position held by General Hoke's division on the 3d. During the war I never saw so many dead Union soldiers on any field. General Hoke's division had not a man killed. The weather was oppressively hot. The blood, burnt powder, and dead bodies produced a stench which cannot be described, and not to be endured long by the living.

General Grant was again moving, not toward Richmond, but away from it, toward the James river; we following, ten days after the battle, crossing to the south side of the Chickahominy, keeping between the Federal army and Richmond, and this tramp watching the movement of General Grant was kept up until the vicinity of Malvern Hill was reached.

I cannot well help breaking the thread of my narrative to tell a little humorous camp story prevalent among our men just after the battle of Cold Harbor. It was claimed to have been told by a Union soldier to some of our men. It ran thus: A private Union soldier who had been in the battle and saw the terrific slaughter, said to his captain, "We have killed and had killed enough men and the war should end, and I know what will end it." The captain inquired, "What?" "Take Richmond," was the response. "Yes," said the captain, "that is what General Grant is trying to do." The soldier insisting that he knew how Richmond could be taken, and the captain pressing him to know, he replied: "Swap Generals!"

CHAPTER XXIII

- **From Malvern Hill to the South of the James.**

- **Engagement at Clay's House.**

- **Bermuda Hundred Line.**

- **Christmas Dinner.**

- **Our Southern Women.**

- **Close of 1864.**

June 15 Pickett's division marched from the vicinity of Malvern Hill up the James, crossing the river the morning of June 16, on a bridge near Dreury's Bluff, then passing over the battlefield of that name, which battle we had fought one month before, reaching the Petersburg turnpike. When near Port Walthall Junction, the head of the column was fired upon by the enemy, who had possession of the road. The division was immediately formed in line of battle on the turnpike, sending out skirmishers, driving the enemy and regaining our first line of works, which had been vacated that morning by the troops having been called to Petersburg. The next day commenced heavy skirmish firing. Company D was on the skirmish line the day before capturing some prisoners, among them an Englishman, who came back saying rather excitedly that he was forced into the army, which nobody believed, for the armies of the enemy were to a considerable extent made up of foreigners. It was often remarked by our men that we were fighting all Yankeedom and the rest of mankind. And this reminds me of the story told by a Confederate of another who like himself had in the battle of the third day at Gettysburg gone over the enemy's line behind the stone fence, reaching a point almost on the crest of Cemetery Ridge. Seeing the mighty host gathered and gathering to envelop the few rebels left, this Confederate cried out, "Do we have to whip the world?" Listening for a moment, he heard a Federal officer say: "Attention, World! By nations right wheel, by states, fire!" He concluded it was time for that poor Confederate to cut dirt, and he stood not on the order of his going.

Let it be remembered that we were now engaged in what is known as the battle of Clay's House. One of our batteries to our left was now throwing shells at the enemy in our front, endeavoring to enfilade their line, during which time I was ordered by Colonel Flowerree to go along the line of the regiment and tell the company commanders to get their men ready for the assault. I had proceeded nearly half way when a misdirected shell from the battery referred to exploded over me, a large fragment grazing my head, burying itself at my feet. Had it struck my head, there would have been one less Sergeant-Major in the Confederate army, and this story would not have been written. A moment later I saw J. B. Young of D Company fall with a severe wound in the head. In a few moments the charge became general, and the enemy's intrenchments were carried. General Lee was riding close in the rear of our battle line at the time of the charge referred to, and meeting one of our regiment badly wounded and being carried out by the litter bearers, said to the wounded man, "I hope, my good fellow, you are not badly hurt."

This charge was the subject of a complimentary letter from General Lee to General Anderson, which is as follows:

"General, I take great pleasure in presenting to you my congratulations upon the conduct of the men of your corps. I believe that they will carry anything they are put against. We tried very hard to stop Pickett's men from capturing the breastworks of the enemy, but couldn't do it. I hope his loss has been small."

This reminds me to say here and now, without intending the least disparagement of others, that the 7th Virginia regiment was never ordered to take the enemy's line that it did not take it, never gave up or lost a position it was ordered to hold, and never left a position or battlefield unless ordered to do so. Once when bodily taken by the Federals and carried into captivity, the reader might consider an exception to the statement just made.

The charge last above referred to was not without its casualties, though I have nothing to show the division, brigade or regimental losses. In the 1st Virginia six men were wounded, and I remember that Sergeant William Parrott of Company I and J. B. Young of Company D were severely and Private William Davis of Company C mortally wounded.

During the remainder of June and for several months following we remained on this Bermuda Hundred line, occasionally shifting position from Howlett House on the James to Swift Creek near the Appomattox, until about the middle of July, then settling down on a high piece of ground behind a skirt of timber midway between Howlett House and Swift Creek. Here we worked hard to strengthen our lines.

Company D now had but a single commissioned officer, Captain Bane. Lieutenant Stone was still a prisoner, Lieutenant Walker had been disabled at Gettysburg and retired, and Lieutenant Mullins had died of the wound received at Howlett House in June. It was on this line that Sergeant T. S. Taylor was elected a lieutenant and E. Z. Yager made orderly sergeant of the company. These selections were well made, and the confidence reposed not misplaced.

Rev. J. Tyler Frazier

At or near this time there appeared on our lines a man representing himself to be a citizen of Alabama, who proposed then to do what could not be done, but in some degree has since been accomplished—to build a machine to navigate the air, carry shells and drop them on the Northern armies, and in their cities. He requested donations from each of the soldiers of one dollar, and of the officers five dollars each to enable him to build his machine. We concluded he was a crank, refused to contribute and the man departed. This fellow was only a little ahead of his time.

At an early hour of July 30th occurred the famous explosion of the mine at Petersburg. Though several miles away, it so shook the earth that the pickets and other men awake at the time felt the shock. The fearful artillery fire which followed convinced us that an important event had occurred. Later in the day we learned what had happened, seeing also a full account of the occurrence in the Richmond papers the next morning. I well remember the comments in the Richmond Examiner (a partisan paper) on the retaking of the line by the division of General Mahone. Describing the slaughter of the Federal soldiers in the crater, it said: "The slaughter was so great that General Mahone sickened at the sight and told his men 'for God's sake to stop,' and the next time we hope General Mahone will shut his eyes." The official report of General Mahone of the retaking of the line and the crater was not furnished by him to his superior officer, but was found by his family among his papers after his death, and published a few years ago. An incident related by the General in his report is worth reproducing here. The General states that his division was on the

Confederate right and a mile or more from where the explosion took place; that the same was not unexpected, but just when and where it would occur no one could certainly tell; that on that morning he was lying on the ground, and on hearing the noise sprang to his feet, looking in every direction to locate from whence the sound came, when he discovered a Confederate soldier at full speed coming towards him. The men along the line were endeavoring to stop him, but without success, so seeing the man was following a path which led near by where the General was standing, he planted himself in the path of the fellow, who was without hat, cap, shoes or coat, and said: "Now stop long enough to tell me what has happened." "Why, Mister," said the soldier, "don't you know that hell has busted?" Evidently this man thought the infernal regions had accidentally exploded.

Between the lines of the two armies as now situated lay a strip of woods, where our men and the Union soldiers were in the habit of meeting to exchange newspapers, coffee and tobacco, now and then playing cards. Our officers on finding out what was going on concluded there was too much familiarity and sought to break it up; so when one of the officers located some of the men engaged in a game of cards with a Union soldier, this Federal was made a prisoner and brought into our lines. The Union soldier was highly indignant at what he considered taking advantage of confidence, for both parties by their acts had waived the fact that they were in the field as deadly foes to each other, and in their hearts our own men had a feeling of the same sort. A little later one of the Union soldiers, thinking to get even, induced a Confederate to meet him between the lines on pretense of exchanging papers, when he attempted his capture, but in the scramble the Confederate proved too much for his captor, dragging him toward our lines, when the Union pickets began firing at the Confederate, who let his man go and escaped. These incidents put a stop for the time being to communication and traffic between the opposing soldiers.

At another time some of our men under the lead of an officer, about daybreak crept over to the Federal skirmish line and between the men in their rifle pits, taking the line in flank and reverse, and raked it for a long distance, bringing out more than a hundred prisoners, including the commanding officer of the line.

How tender the fellow feeling of one soldier for another, though on opposite sides, is shown by the following incident: The Union soldiers, well knowing that we were scarce of food, at dusk one day called to one of our men, "Say, Johnnie, are you hungry?" "Yes," replied the Confederate, "have had but little to eat for two or three days," to which the Union soldier said, "Bring your haversack over here and I will take you to the sutler and fill it," but the Confederate demurred, giving as his reason that he was afraid he would be captured. Being assured, however, upon the honor of a soldier that he should have a safe return, he went, and the Union soldier filled his haversack and returned him safely to our lines.

The enemy was reported shifting about in our front beyond and behind the timber, where we could not see him, and supposing he might be preparing for an attack upon us, by order of the Colonel, with Pitts of Company C and Crawford of Company D, I went to the front, outside our pickets, where I ran upon a scouting or observation party of the enemy, by whom we were fired on, and came near being gobbled up, but escaped and returned within our lines. We had a close call.

Wishing to visit some friends in Captain David A. French's artillery company, then stationed near Chaffin's Bluff north of the James, three miles away, I obtained a pass and put off on September 28, spending the night with friends, finding myself the next morning almost in a hornet's nest, for on the morning of the 29th the Federal troops advanced and captured Fort Harrison, a mile to the front of the camp of French's company. I followed the battery, witnessing the fight, in which the Federals advancing from Fort Harrison were repulsed. French lost several men, among them Adam Johnston, killed. I did not tarry long, but set out for my command, meeting on the way a part of our division, the 24th Virginia regiment among them, on their way to reinforce our troops in front of Fort Harrison, where they were defeated in the attempt to recapture the fort.

As already stated, the line from the Howlett House to Swift Creek, some three miles in length, was held by Pickett's division, four thousand strong; the skirmish line or rifle pits of the opposing forces were close together, say 30 yards apart, and the main lines but a few hundred yards away. Our line was so thin and so drawn out that when thrown into the trenches it made scarcely more than a strong skirmish line. We were frequently in the trenches expecting attack, and the morning following the battle of Winchester we were sure the enemy was coming, but he was content with firing a shotted salute. At this time desertions from our ranks, as well as from the ranks of the enemy, became more frequent and punishment more sure. Numbers of the enemy came into our lines and were sent to the rear and the same course was pursued by the enemy with men deserting from us. Now and then a man instead of going over to the enemy would go home and hide and when caught would be tried and shot. This happened to a mere boy, a member of Company B of our regiment, who was executed October 18, 1864. At this distance from the war, a half century, such a thing may shock the reader, but war at best is a horrible thing and discipline must be enforced. It was not strange that some men deserted and went home. Many had families dependent on them for food and support. The soldier's pay for a month, in Confederate currency, with the necessaries of life advanced to enormous figures, would not buy a half bushel of wheat for his family. The cry of his children for bread reached his ears and this was more than his heart could bear. He became dissatisfied—anxious for the suffering ones at home. He was willing to bare his breast to the storm, and undergo the hardships and privations of camp life and the dangers of the battlefield, if he knew his wife and children were kept from starving, but their appeals for food moved him; he would obtain leave to go if he could, otherwise he would go without leave; but it will be seen if this were permitted the army would soon be depleted, and the cause we were fighting for lost. The dilemma was therefore a trying one to many a good man.

The Colonel of the 7th regiment, having instructions to capture a prisoner to obtain certain information wanted, and going to the skirmish line, where Company D under Captain Bane was on picket, instructed him to secure such prisoner. Bane called for volunteers for this enterprise and three men responded, among them John W. East, who agreed to capture the prisoner by playing the role of deserter, which he did by going over to the enemy. The Federal picket called our men up next morning and told them East had deserted the night before. This was no less than a ruse on John's part to desert and go over to the side of the enemy.

Among the inducements offered by the Federal officers to our men to desert was that if their homes were within the Federal lines they should be sent home and protected or given government employment at good wages, but love of cause and country were more potent than all the inducements offered on the other side.

A. L. Sumner, of Company D, an illiterate man, heard someone read from a Richmond paper one morning in November, 1864, that Mr. Lincoln had been re-elected president of the United States, and had called for a large number of additional men. Sumner sat with his head bowed, when a comrade approaching and seeing that something was troubling him, inquired the cause. Sumner responded, "Don't you know that Abe Lincoln is re-elected and has called for a million men, and that Jeff Davis says war to the knife? What shall we do?"—A pertinent inquiry.

Christmas, 1864, was approaching and extensive preparations were being made by city, town and country to furnish the army of Northern Virginia a Christmas dinner, the women taking the lead—God bless them! The newspapers urged the movement forward, committees were appointed to collect and forward the good things to the soldiers. The papers proclaimed that Virginia, devastated as she was by an invading host, was yet able to feed her soldiers; that the cattle upon a thousand hills were hers. Though the cattle were not there, the day came, and with it a bountiful supply which made us glad, and we thanked our benefactors and took courage.

The credit for our Christmas dinner was due the women. In every movement for the uplift and betterment of our race, and in every worthy cause, woman is the first to espouse, the last to forsake. Having once fixed her affections upon the object of our cause, her love therefor became as fast and enduring as the rock-ribbed hills. The wives, mothers and sisters of the men gave their husbands, sons and brothers to the cause, suffered untold agony and sorrows, depriving themselves of every comfort, to the end that the soldiers in the field might be clothed and fed. For them no sacrifice was too great. The Southern woman, accustomed to the indulgences and refinements of life, became familiar with the coarsest of personal apparel, and a scarcity of food which she had never known, and she bore these things without a murmur. She followed the plow, reaped the grain, took it to the mill, nursed the sick and wounded, buried the dead, and rendered thousands of kindnesses to our suffering soldiers, only recorded in the hearts and memories of the recipients of these loving deeds, and of Him whose eye is never shut. In the days of "reconstruction," when men were awe stricken, not knowing whither to look or what to do, these women stood with resolute trust in God, giving words of encouragement to the sterner sex; and became, as it were, the strong vine entwined around the sturdy tree when shaken by the storm. These Southern women were the only portion of our people who never surrendered. They are today the purest type of Anglo-Saxon womanhood on the face of the earth.

Memorial Day originated with our Southern women, whose custom it is to strew flowers, mementoes of their undying love, on the graves of the gray and the blue alike. They are the guardians of the graves of our noble dead.

"This place of burial is

   Hallowed by woman's prayers;

A nobler epitaph than this

   Could not be theirs."

Things now began to look dark. General Sherman was marching through Georgia to the sea; Hood's army had been defeated at Nashville. The situation was grave in the extreme. With all this came strange presentiments. The dark clouds that had been for some time overhanging us were settling down. The patriotism, enthusiasm and untold sacrifices of the past four years seemed all for naught, and our men could not be required to shoulder a heavier cross than was now the lot of the Confederate soldiers. But a patriotic people and a valiant soldiery might yet accomplish success, looking we were, but in vain, for foreign intervention, or something else to turn up. If to satisfy the Northern people and gain our separate existence meant to give up slavery, the army was ready to see it abolished. In fact, the great bulk of the army was ready to make almost any sacrifice required for independent and separate government. Our forefathers had resisted British tyranny, we were resisting Northern aggression upon the sovereignty and reserved rights of the States of the Confederacy.

Dark and discouraging as were these days, the spirit of the army was yet unbroken, and the men were willing to fight it out, although it appeared but a question of time when we should all go down.

Thus closed the year of 1864, and to us it seemed final overthrow must come, for our foe was growing stronger, we weaker. Our star was surely on the wane.

CHAPTER XXIV

- **Religion in the Army.**

- **Doctors Pryor, Fontaine, Stiles.**

- **General Pendleton.**

- **Young Men's Christian Association.**

- **Frazier, Our Preaching-Fighting Chaplain.**

My presentation of the subject of religion in the army will necessarily be confined to the command to which I belonged and what came under my personal observation. When the call to arms was made in 1861, the sentiment of our people was a solemn appeal to God for the rectitude of our intentions and purposes, an appeal to the God of battles for His abiding presence and blessing upon our undertaking. Nearly every step taken was witnessed by religious services. Our whole Southland was permeated with the spirit and teachings of the Bible. The brave people of our land believed in God—indeed, the foundations of their state government were based upon their faith in the Author of their lives and liberty. This was no mere phantom. Most of our great leaders were Christian men, who feared and worshipped God.

At the beginning of the war we had many wild, profane men who had joined the army, but from this it must not be inferred that our camps were scenes of vulgarity, and profanity. With but few exceptions, after the first year or so of the war, there was never an army freer from vice, immorality and anger. That which in the beginning would have been offensive and insulting, and probably brought the parties to blows, was now passed by. The men had come to understand each other's temperaments. They had lived, associated, marched, fought, slept and eaten together too long, had suffered in common too many hardships, enduring the same privations, not to know each other's Christian convictions. They were therefore "Souls that had but a single thought, and hearts that beat as one." They were, with a true Christian spirit, ready to bear each other's burdens, care for each other when sick or wounded, comfort each other when in trouble and distress, and therefore the better prepared to entertain the "King of Peace."

Many of the men of my company, some of whom I have already mentioned, were Christians when they entered the army, and by their example and character exerted a wholesome influence for good. When resting in camp, these men remembered their vows, conducting religious exercises in their quarters before retiring at night. On Sunday we usually had services, led by the Chaplains, who were zealous Christians, and patriotic men, even going into battle with us. One, Dr. Granberry, chaplain of the 11th Virginia, and after the war a Methodist Bishop, was wounded in the battle of Seven Pines. In the absence of the regular chaplain, Brother Frazier, acting as such, preached to us.

Near the close of 1862, and throughout the greater part of the year of 1863, a religious spirit seemed to possess the army; at least this was true of our command. Christians had great reason to thank God and take courage when they thought on the remarkable progress the gospel was making in the camp. Thousands of young men embraced religion. While churches at home were languishing, the gospel was moving forward with marvelous strides among the soldiers in the field. Indeed, what could be more fitting, with real men accustomed daily to witnessing carnage and death. There was therefore much comfort to the men in having the gospel successfully preached and the standard of the Master borne aloft in the trenches, in sight of the enemy, even within musket and cannon's range. At the administration of the baptismal ordinance, the banks of the Rappahannock, Rapidan and the James and other streams resounded with the songs of praise. Our chaplains often proclaimed the glad tidings amid the noise of the booming cannon and rattle of musketry. This spirit was caught by our division at Taylorsville in the spring of 1863, when Dr. Pryor of Petersburg preached for us for several days in succession, hundreds professing-faith in Christ. The whole camp was one religious gathering, and all men seemed greatly interested. There was a grand and glorious awakening. Many in the Spring of 1863 found the blessed Savior precious, to their souls and rejoiced in His love, I among the number.

When on the march to Gettysburg, halting for a day or more, religious exercises were conducted; scarcely would the column halt at night and supper over before the sacred songs began; around those singing would gather the soldiers in large numbers, the chaplain, or someone else, conducting the exercises. This was continued during the fall of 1863, in Culpeper, on the Rapidan, again at Taylorsville, in North Carolina, in Virginia, near Hanover Junction, around Cold Harbor, Malvern Hill, and on the south of the James, where Drs. Stiles and Fontaine were occasionally with us. The latter, Rev. P. H. Fontaine, a minister of the Baptist Church, visited us in September, 1864, preaching successfully for several days; many desiring baptism going to a small branch close by our line in a ravine, where a dam was constructed, furnishing sufficient water to bury a man in baptism, as was our Savior in the Jordan, a comforting scene to many wearied and homesick hearts. On Monday, September 12, 1864, Mr. Fontaine baptized a large number of soldiers on their profession of faith—

how many I do not recollect, but of our company two, Tim P. Darr and the writer. Darr became a Methodist preacher, dying last year (1913) in the State of Kentucky.

The army of Northern Virginia by the close of the year 1864 had in large measure become a band of Christian soldiers, God-fearing men. Amid the trying scenes, shoeless, in tattered rags, hungry, chilled by the cold, they gathered, if opportunity offered, and on bended knees asked God to comfort their homes and little ones, to bless our arms with success and to crown our efforts with early peace and stable government.

The venerable Doctor Stiles and General Pendleton—the latter an Episcopal minister and the chief of artillery of the army of Northern Virginia—occasionally preached to the troops. Through the instrumentality of J. Tyler Frazier there was organized a Young Men's Christian Association, of Kemper's brigade, into which was largely incorporated all the professing Christians in the brigade. It met regularly when not on the march, and among the articles of the constitution was one providing that if any member of the Association should desert or absent himself from his command without leave, he should be excluded. The Association stood pledged to discourage desertions or insubordination, and on the other hand to encourage obedience and fidelity to cause and country; by all means within its power to diffuse religious thought and morality throughout the brigade. While on the Bermuda Hundred line, the men built a church in which religious services were held, and which was also used as a place of entertainment.

J. Tyler Frazier, whose name has been frequently mentioned in this narrative, deserves a more extended notice. Mr. Frazier was born in Giles County, Virginia, in the year 1840, embracing Christianity at an early age. His early opportunities for acquiring an education were quite limited, but being a man of exceptionally good sense, a preacher when he entered the army—the company chaplain, did his duty nobly and well. By precept and example upon all proper occasions he endeavored to impress upon the men the importance of living a Christian life. Notice has already been taken of some of his messmates, Taylor, Henderson, Fortner, Darr and others, God-fearing men. Mr. Frazier preached whenever opportunity offered, not only to the company, regiment and brigade, but to the people of the region roundabout. The chaplaincy of the regiment being vacant, the Young Men's Christian Association desired the appointment of Mr. Frazier to the vacancy, naming a committee consisting of Thomas S. Taylor (who died in this year, 1914), Edward Hoge (now dead), and David E. Johnston, to take up the matter with the Colonel, but our mission failed because the commander felt that a man could not be spared from the ranks who was so good a soldier as Brother Frazier. We secured, however, the privilege for

Mr. Frazier to preach where and when he pleased, having his musket and accouterments transported in headquarters wagon, the only requirement being demanded that he should take his gun and go into battle. Mr. Frazier was as useful as chaplain without a commission as with it, for he still continued to preach, pray, march and fight, to exhort and encourage men to do their duty to God and their country. He was spared and returned home, entered the regular Methodist ministry of the Southern Methodist Church, has been a presiding elder, a successful preacher, and still lives to bless humanity. He now resides on his fine estate near Chilhowie, Virginia, preaching regularly, esteemed and highly respected by his brethren, old comrades, friends and neighbors.

In closing this chapter, I may be permitted with genuineness of purpose to add a final word to the sons and daughters, descendants of the noble Confederate soldiers of Virginia, whom I deeply loved, and of whom I have endeavored, though with much imperfection, to write in these pages.

Another warfare is today calling you to the field. I have seen much of life and know the fruits of vice and shame, the danger of gilded pitfalls and deceptive traps which are set for you and your children. I beg of you not to think of this as idle talk on my part. You are in imminent danger of the captivity from which there is no return. For your safety the Great Leader is calling you to join His forces, to enlist in His cause. This Leader has never known defeat, has never lost a soldier. If you are in His service, your name is enrolled on high. If you are faithful, you will not be overlooked nor forgotten. If you have not given Him your life and everything belonging to you, I beg you not to delay. Your father obeyed our country's call in 1861. It is fitting now that you obey the gospel call into the noblest army earth has ever known. More than once did I look into the faces of your noble sires, as they stood at Sharpsburg, Gettysburg and Cold Harbor, in defense of the right. I think of the courage with which they followed the old flag, and I love you for their sakes. I pray God that each of you may honor the memory of those fathers by being brave and steadfast soldiers of the Cross; that you may have a place in the ranks of that great army composed of the pure and the good on earth and in heaven.

CHAPTER XXV

- **From January, 1865, to Close of Battle of Five Forks.**
- **Gloomy Outlook at the Opening of the Year.**
- **The Peace Commissioners.**
- **Spirit of the Army.**
- **A. S. Fry as Regimental Clerk and Historian.**
- **Trouble in Company D.**
- **Activity Within the Federal Lines.**
- **General Pendleton's Speech.**
- **Early's Small Force Defeated at Waynesboro.**
- **Sheridan's Raid.**

While near Swift Creek, A. L. Fry of Company D was appointed clerk and regimental historian, making a complete roll of the men of the regiment, noting their services, for which he received a short furlough. The record made by Fry was filed away in Richmond, but unfortunately was destroyed by fire on the evacuation of the city by the Confederate troops. This was indeed a calamity, for such a record would now, after half a century, be of priceless value. The record of many a poor fellow which was thus lost cannot be had anywhere else.

We changed position from near Swift Creek to the Howlett House on the James in January, 1865, where we erected rude shacks of timber and earth which furnished slight shelter from the pelting storms. Near the middle of the month the weather softened, and we were enabled to get out and engage in ball and other games, which gave us exercise and good appetites, though ordinarily we were ready to eat anything we could get, for at that time our daily allowance was one-fourth pound of bacon and one pint of coarse cornmeal, with occasionally a little sugar, rice, beans or peas.

The period was still gloomy. Fort McAllister had fallen, Savannah was in the hands of the enemy, Charleston and Fort Fisher seriously threatened; Hood's army had been wrecked and driven out of Tennessee; General Sherman was preparing to march through the Carolinas. General Grant had seized the Petersburg and Weldon railroad and was now threatening to strike the south side and Richmond and Danville road—the latter being the only remaining line connecting Richmond with the Southern states, over which our supplies must be drawn. The situation was therefore serious. This was fully realized by the men in the ranks. Vastly superior territory, unlimited supplies, and a call for 300,000 new troops in the North were calculated to produce discouragement in the hearts of men who had from the first been fighting against heavy odds. Desertions became more frequent; many men were absent without leave, on account of needy families and other causes, and were in no hurry to return. All these things were discussed by the soldiers in their huts. The army of Northern Virginia now consisted of less than fifty thousand poorly equipped, poorly clad, poorly fed men, who had marched and countermarched, charged and fought a foe two or three times their number for nearly four long, dreadful years. It was little wonder, therefore, that depression came to the noble army of Northern Virginia, which then held the toe line from a point north of Fort Harrison to the vicinity of Hatcher's Run to the south, more than thirty-five miles—in many places little more than a good skirmish line, which the enemy was able to confront with full lines, and yet overreaching our flanks, and was continuing to extend his lines. Why General Grant did not cut loose from his base at City Point and swing around the Confederate right, shutting the army up in Petersburg and Richmond, is a military problem I will not endeavor to solve.

I was in Richmond in January, 1865, and saw bread selling at $2.00 for a small loaf; a pound of soda for $12.00; a calico dress pattern, $25.00, a gold dollar commanding $60.00 in Confederate currency.

The mission of the Confederate "Peace Commissioners" had been a failure, and a great disappointment to the soldiers, who saw plainly nothing short of a bitter fight to the end. Public meetings of the men were held in many of the commands in the army, resolutions adopted, expressing regret at the failure of the Peace Conference, reaffirming their faith in the justness of our cause, and rededicating themselves to the defense thereof, resolving to fight to the end. Surely heroism and desperation equal to this cannot be found in the annals of history. With this situation confronting them, they demanded that all absentees should be returned to their places, all able bodied men should be required to take the field, and that every step possible should be taken to strengthen the army, even to the arming of the negroes—a thing which should have been done long before this.

In order to give some conception of the feeling and sentiment which then pervaded the soldiers, I here insert an extract from a letter written a friend in February, 1865, in which I say: "There is nothing left us but to fight it out; the cry is for war—war to the knife. If the people at home will support the army and drive all skulkers and absentees to the front, all will be right."

Amid the darkness and gloom surrounding us, some of the men would have fun. I well remember that W. D. Peters, of D Company, a wit and wag, having around him several of his comrades, inquired as to how the Southern Confederacy was bounded. One answered, "North by the United States, south by the Gulf of Mexico, east by the Atlantic Ocean, west by the Rocky Mountains." Peters insisted this to be a mistake, saying that "we were surrounded by Yankees!"

The general sentiment in the army favored freeing all negroes who would take arms and fight for the country. To this, singularly enough, came opposition from men who did not and never had owned a slave. The proposition to arm the negroes did not find favor with the politicians, but they were finally forced to yield, late in the Spring of 1865, on the eve of the retreat of the army of Northern Virginia from the Richmond-Petersburg lines.

While on the lines near Howlett House, a squad went out between the skirmish lines to gather fuel; among the number was Adam Thompson, who had so large a foot that special requisition had to be made to get shoes big enough for him; the shoes for Adam had to be made to order. On the occasion referred to, Adam deserted to the enemy, when a Union soldier called out, "Jonnnie! Have you another man over there three feet across the back and who wears a number two shoe—two hides to the shoe?"

I here relate an incident happening on this line while at the Howlett House, which caused much grief, growing out, as I believe, of misinformation and misunderstanding, whereby three of the best soldiers of Company D—A. J. Thompson, Harry Snidow and J. C. Hughes—were arrested upon a charge of encouraging insubordination and mutiny, of which they were convicted and sentenced to be shot, and pending the approval of General Lee (which was never had, so far as I know), were incarcerated in "Castle Thunder" in Richmond, from which they were only released by the Union army on entering the city April 3, 1865. In the opinion of the writer, who knew these three men, all sergeants, through and through, this proceeding was excessive and unwarranted. Surely three long years of untiring devotion and loyalty to the cause for which we fought should be counted worth something.

General Pendleton, the chief of artillery of the army, visited our lines the middle of March and made a speech, in which he said, "The time is rapidly approaching for the opening of the campaign, and that man Grant over there means mischief. Only with a union of strong arms and brave hearts can we hope to win. Pack your haversacks and be ready to move." There was now great activity within the lines of the enemy; the whistle of the locomotive, the inclination and the action of the enemy to crowd us, all pointed to an early movement, but the question confronted us—What are we to do? Can we get away and how far? Not a mule nor horse that can pull a hundred pounds five miles through the mud. It was suggested, let us go south and join General Joe Johnston, unite forces with him, whip Grant and then Sherman. Some said one thing, some another, but all agreed that if Richmond had to be given up, it were better it had been abandoned the fall before, when our transportation was in better shape and our army numerically stronger, and General Grant's not in such good condition, not yet having recovered from its bloody campaign from the Rapidan to Petersburg, and not so confident as now.

Brigadier-General David E. Johnston and Aid-de-Camp D. E. J. Wilson

In March, 1865, at night, our division was withdrawn from the lines, Mahone's division taking our place. We were hurried up to Richmond to the outer intrenchments north of the city to meet the Federal General Sheridan's cavalry corps of 10,000 men, which a few days before had overwhelmed the little band of about 1500 men of General Early in the valley near Waynesboro, and were now rapidly approaching Richmond by way of Charlottesville. Near Ashland Corse's brigade had a brisk skirmish with Sheridan's advance. It was apparent that General Sheridan had no thought of attacking Richmond (he was never known to attack unless he had the advantage) but had crossed the Chickahominy and was making his way to join the main army south of the James.

CHAPTER XXVI

- **South of the James.**

- **Battles of Dinwiddie and Five Forks.**

- **The Retreat.**

We were hastened through Richmond and to the south of the James, marching to the South Side railroad west of Petersburg, thence on to Sutherland Station, reaching there at 9 P.M., Wednesday, March 29, and going forward through an all night's rain, arriving at the White Oak road at dawn, where a portion of General Bushrod Johnson's division was in line of battle, with a brisk skirmish progressing in front. Three brigades of Pickett's division, Corse's, Stuart's and Terry's, with Ransom's and Wallace's—the last two now consolidated under General Ransom—extended the battle line of Johnson's division to the right. Here we remained until the middle of the afternoon, a heavy rain falling during the greater part of the time, our skirmishers having an occasional brush with the enemy. The column then moved forward along the road in the direction of Five Forks, skirmishing front and flank, reaching the Forks at sunset; without halting, Corse's brigade, and the 1st and 7th regiments of Terry's, advanced, driving the dismounted cavalry of the enemy through and out of the woods and across the open country beyond; then returning to the Forks, lay down under a pelting rain upon the wet ground until morning, thus in line ready to fight or march.

It was 10 A.M., Friday, March 31, that the advance began in the direction of Dinwiddie Court House, the cavalry in our front fighting at every step, crossing Chamberlain Run, and being driven back, as the infantry was unable to afford them help on account of the swollen condition of the stream. Finally, at the remains of an old mill on the Run, the infantry succeeded in getting over, in the face of a sharp fire from the enemy, with whom, as soon as across the stream, we kept up a running fight until near sunset. When near the Court House we encountered a large body of the enemy's dismounted cavalry formed across the road prepared to oppose our further advance. A Federal battery of artillery in their center commanded the ground over which the advance had to be made, but we made a successful charge, sweeping the field, the enemy retiring in confusion, leaving their dead and wounded, we occupying the battlefield until nearly 1 o'clock next morning.

In this engagement, known as the battle of Dinwiddie, the famous cavalry officer, General Phil Sheridan, with all his brag, was scared out of his boots—calling that night on General Grant for an army corps of infantry to help him out of the scrape, although he already had more men on the field than the Confederates who were assailing him.

Humanity, the crowning grace of the brave soldier, secured for the wounded—the enemy's as well as our own—all the care and attention we were able to give them. Our loss had not been heavy, especially was it small in our regiment—none in Company D. General Terry's horse was struck by a cannon shot, which caused it to fall with the General, giving him quite a severe injury.[5]

Near midnight, or a little later, March 31, the Confederates retired to Five Forks, five miles away, taking position in battle line, and hastily throwing up temporary breastworks of logs. W. H. F. Lee's cavalry was on the right, then the infantry brigades, Corse, Terry, Steuart, Ransom-Wallace, in the order named, with a portion of Fitzhugh Lee's cavalry under General Munford on the left. Terry's brigade held the ground immediately on the right of the Forks, with the left of the 7th Virginia resting at the Forks, at which was posted three guns of Colonel William Pegram's Virginia battalion of artillery. The enemy did not appear in force in our front until nearly 10 A.M. next day.

Five Forks is situated in a thickly wooded, flat, wet country, and gets its name from the crossing of two country roads at right angles, with the deflection of another road bisecting one of these angles; the last place that a general with a small force would desire to meet a large force, or select his ground upon which to fight a defensive battle, because it was in an open country. This position could be easily turned, and a small force easily isolated from the main army at Petersburg, which the enemy, in fact, did by throwing General Warren's infantry corps, nearly 15,000 strong, against the Confederate left, between it and the right wing of our army. This point could only have been necessary to hold to protect the South Side railroad, and for this reason may have been regarded strategic, but it could not be held by a small force, if an enemy in superior numbers chose to turn it, who had the advantage of approach from two or more of the five roads converging there.

Privates Crawford and Dudley of Company D were on the skirmish line. After several unsuccessful attempts by the Federal skirmishers to drive in ours, they concluded to try something stronger. In the meantime Crawford had his musket stock at the small part thereof severed and he came back to the main line, procured another, and returned to his place with the skirmishers. By this time the Federal battle line, composed partly of dismounted cavalry, was advancing, and soon overran our skirmishers, killing, wounding and capturing nearly the whole of them, coming with a rush at our main line, by which they were severely punished and repelled. These attacks were several times repeated along our whole brigade front, each time being repulsed with loss to the enemy and with little to us. Warren's infantry corps, having placed itself near the middle of the afternoon around and beyond the Confederate left, advancing boldly struck Ransom's and Wallace's brigades in flank, doubling them up and pushing them to us in the center. Steuart's and Terry's brigades now moved out of their intrenched line and with a fierce, determined fight met the oncoming battle against more than 15,000 with less than two thousand. In the nature of things this could not and did not last long, but it did last until the moon was up and the evening shades had fallen. This scribe, it will be remembered, was still only a boy, and remembers distinctly Colonel Flowerree saying, "Now, boys, in marching away follow that moon." This because we were in a country unknown to us or to our commander. Our brigade was in conflict with Ayers' Federal division, which was massed in column, firing over each other and too high, thus accounting for our small regimental and brigade loss in killed and wounded.

Before being withdrawn from our intrenched line to meet the flank attack of Warren's corps, Colonel Pegram of the artillery fell on the left of our regiment, mortally wounded. The 7th regiment, numbering less than 300 men, under the fearless Colonel Flowerree, was thrown into the breach to stem the tide, but after a few minutes of close, almost hand-to-hand struggle, it left the field, not however, before being ordered three times by the Colonel to do so.

In the woods where we were fighting it was getting dark, the moon beginning to shine. My position as Sergeant-Major was on the left of the regiment, which I occupied during the fierce contest. Seeing the regiment move rapidly by the right flank and to the rear, but in good order, I stood for a moment reflecting whether I should leave or take the chances of death or becoming a prisoner. Choosing the former, and passing the road over which we had fought our way a few minutes before, I found myself with two Confederates, who were a little in advance of me, and proceeding but a short distance we found ourselves plump up against the lines of Federal cavalry. A Sergeant demanded our surrender, the Confederate nearest him threw down his gun; the one next to me turned and said, "What shall we do?" I still had the carbine I had picked up the day before in the battle near Dinwiddie, but no ammunition, and without replying to the question or dropping my gun, but keeping my eyes fixed on the sergeant, who was separated by a small space from his comrades as well as from me, I observed that his cap had been knocked off by the limb of a pine bush under which he had ridden, and that his attention was fixed upon an effort to get his cap. Just then seeing an opening where the Federal regiments joined, I darted through, amidst a shower of bullets, the wind and heat of some of them being felt distinctly in my face. The reader may easily imagine the speed made just then by a Confederate Sergeant-Major. In less than two hundred yards beyond, I overtook my command forming across the road.

Here Generals Pickett, Corse, Steuart, Ransom and Colonel Mayo were urging the men to get quickly into line, Pickett in the midst of the fire behaving with his usual gallantry and coolness. In the middle of the road stood the ensign of the 1st Virginia regiment, with his colors and guard, with Gentry and his Glee Club, singing, "Rally Round the Flag, Boys, Rally Once Again"—and rally they did, although badly mixed, but in a few minutes partial order was restored, not a moment too soon, for the enemy was coming. The position now held was not more than four hundred yards from the Forks. As yet, the enemy had gained but little ground, though he had captured a large number of prisoners, principally of Ransom's, Wallace's and Steuart's brigades, and of the 11th and the 24th Virginia of Terry's brigade. The enemy now bore down heavily upon our right front, advancing through an open field, we being in a skirt of woods, from which we sent into them a murderous volley. The smoke clearing away, it was revealed that his whole line had been shattered, large numbers of his dead and wounded on the ground, the living fleeing in full haste. In the meantime the enemy had thrown a heavy force around both the Confederate flanks, threatening to envelop us between his columns, and cutting our line of retreat, forming something of the shape of a horse-shoe, we being in the toe, having the heel open, as the only chance to get out. This gap in the heel was much broadened by a charge of the Confederate cavalry on the right. It was now dark, the command badly scattered, and almost surrounded by the enemy. We moved to the rear as rapidly as possible, and those remaining not killed, wounded or captured, made their way across the South Side railroad, where camp was made.

This was one of the most fiercely and best contested battles of the war, disparity of numbers considered. It can be safely and truthfully asserted by those present who witnessed what occurred that never were troops placed in a more trying situation—outflanked on both wings, attacked front flank and rear, by a force fully four times their numbers, in a comparatively flat, open country, away from supports, without shelter save rude log breastworks, hastily thrown up, occupied for a short time during the fight, which was as close as fearless men could make it. There was no panic, for the men rallied and fought again and again, until dark, when the enemy desisted. Much of the fighting was so close that there was a question as to who would be the victors.

General Grant in his Memoirs says of this battle: "It was dusk when our troops under Sheridan went over the parapets of the enemy. The two armies were mingled together there for a time in such manner that it was almost a question which one was going to demand the surrender of the other."

It now appears that the army of the enemy on the field numbered above 26,000, while I am satisfied we could not have had exceeding 8000 men at the opening of the battle. We had the consolidated brigades of Ransom and Wallace, about 1000; Steuart's brigade, about 1000; Corse's brigade, about 1100; Terry's brigade, about 900; cavalry, 3500, and artillerists 300; Rosser's cavalry division guarding the trains, not in the battle.

The Federal loss was 124 killed and 706 wounded; the Confederate loss, 450 killed, 750 wounded. The Confederates lost four guns, eleven colors and 3244 prisoners, a loss which the reader will see from statements made was by us sorely felt.

I do not know the division, brigade or regimental losses, but they were severe in the regiment, while Company D lost but six men—Crawford, Dudley, Sumner and Mullins, as prisoners. John A. Hale and William D. Peters severely wounded, both got off the field. Captain Bane, Lieutenant Taylor and the following men: Bolton, Crawford, Darr, Dudley, Eaton, Frazier, Fry, Gordon, Hale (J. A.), Henderson, Hurt (J. J.), Meadows, Mullins, Minnich (C), Minnich (G. A.), Peters, Shannon, Stafford, Sumner, Suthern, Wiley, Yager and the writer—25—were all the men and officers of Company D in this battle of Five Forks.

In Warren's swing around our left he had killed, wounded and captured a large part of our dismounted cavalry on that wing, practically the whole of the brigades of Ransom and Wallace and a large part of Steuart's. After this capture we could not have had more than 4500 men left, who kept up and maintained the fight until 6 o'clock P.M. It was simply a yielding to overwhelming numbers, and the strangest thing of all is that we were not all captured or killed. It was within the power of the Federals at any time after 4 o'clock P.M. to have made prisoners of us all, and nothing but bad Federal generalship and the protection of God saved us, for the Union army were brave enough. There is no doubt about Sheridan's men fighting; they were men many of whom for gallant conduct had been taken from other arms of the service and placed in the cavalry. They were brave, reckless, and withal generous foes.

In closing this account of the battle of Five Forks I here insert some extracts from General Longstreet's book, "Bull Run to Appomattox." Speaking of Warren's flank movement and after Ransom's and Wallace's brigades had been broken up, he says: "The brigades of Steuart and Terry changed front and received the rolling battle ... the Confederate brigades were pushed back to their extreme right, where in turn Corse's brigade changed front to receive the march." Again: "The position was not of General Pickett's choosing, and from his orders he assumed he would be reinforced. His execution was all that a skilful commander could apply.... Though taken by surprise, there was no panic in any part of the command; brigade after brigade changed front to the left and received the overwhelming battle as it rolled on until it was crushed back to the next, before it could deploy out to aid the front—or flank attack, until the last brigade of the brave Corse changed and stood alone on the left.... It is not claiming too much for that grand division to say that, aided by the brigades of Ransom and Wallace, they could not have been dislodged from their intrenched position by parallel battle, even by the great odds against them. As it was, Ayer's division, staggered under the pelting blows that it met, and Crawford's drifted from the blows against it, until it thus found the key of the battle away beyond the Confederate limits. In generalship Pickett was not a bit below the 'gay rider.' His defensive battle was better organized, and it is possible that he would have gained the day if his cavalry had been diligent in giving information of the movements of the enemy."

----

[5]

On account of Gen'l. Terry's injury, Col. Jo Mayo of the Third Regiment was in command of the brigade at Five Forks.

CHAPTER XXVII

- **The Retreat.**

- **Battle of Sailor's Creek.**

- **Captured.**

Early in the morning of Sunday, April 2, we marched from our camp near South Side railway into the main road leading west to Amelia Court House. Reaching this road, we found portions of Heth's and Wilcox's divisions moving along the same, by whom we were informed that our lines around Petersburg had been broken and they cut off from the rest of the army.

We pushed on that day, learning en route that General A. P. Hill had been killed before Petersburg. We went into camp near Deep Creek, hungry and conscious of loss, both in the breaking of the lines at Petersburg and in the death of sturdy, gallant A. P. Hill—and still there was no murmuring.

During the forenoon on Monday the enemy's cavalry came up with our rear guard, when some brisk skirmishing occurred. We passed Deep Creek near 2 P.M., the enemy pressing closely. Late in the evening we received a scanty supply of rations, the first since March 29—four days. Beyond Deep Creek a short distance we went into camp; moving next morning on the road to Amelia Court House, but the enemy had been there ahead of us, had made an attack upon a wagon train, and were driven off by the teamsters and stragglers, leaving their dead and some of their wounded on the streets. Here we heard of the evacuation of Richmond. This, though looked for, brought deep gloom over not a few of the men, who for more than three years had not faltered in hope of ultimate success. From the time Amelia Court House was left at noon on the 4th until Thursday, the 6th, at the close of the battle of Sailor's Creek, there was scarcely an hour, day or night, that we were not engaged in skirmishing with the enemy. They were on the flank, and everywhere, after our beleaguered troops. We were forced to halt and form line of battle, once or more a square, to prevent capture. The march was necessarily slow on account of the wagon and artillery trains, which moved at a snail's pace through the mud, drawn by famished animals, which had had but little food for days. While soldiers may live for a time on enthusiasm, mules and horses must have corn or oats. As for ourselves, we were without food, save a little parched corn, when we could stop long enough to parch it; otherwise we took it raw, shelling it from the cob and eating it as we marched. The small ration issued to us at Deep Creek had only been sufficient for one square meal. Many of the men were overcome with fatigue, hunger and want of sleep, some actually going to sleep walking along, stumbling and falling in the road. No food was to be had in the country along the road upon which we were marching, as the people had been stripped of everything in the way of food by those who had preceded us. It was unsafe to venture far from the command on account of the enemy's cavalry now on all the roads, and many of our men were made prisoners by going away from the line of march in search of food. We halted for rest but once during the night of Wednesday, the 5th, then only for a few minutes, in line of battle, for the enemy was close upon us.

It was the general expression that if all of our marchings, sufferings, hardships, privations and sacrifices for all of the preceding years of the war were summed up, shaken together and pressed down, they would not equal those we were now undergoing on this tramp.

At daylight on Thursday, April 6, a point was reached near Sailor's Creek, a small tributary of the Appomattox, a short distance from High Bridge, and probably ten miles from Farmville. The marching of our depleted and exhausted forces for the past two days had been conducted during the day by throwing out skirmishers on both flanks, and calling them in at dark, our rear now being cared for by the troops of General Ewell. The skirmishers in front and on the flank became actively engaged at sunrise, the balls from the enemy's sharpshooters whistling over and among the men of the regiment. Here I saw for the first and last time General Henry A. Wise, a tall, slender, gray-haired man, straight as an arrow, apparently vigorous for a man of his years. We were now to fight our last engagement—the battle of Sailor's Creek.

The skirmishing now grew more animated, we expecting every moment to be attacked, but the enemy was merely attracting our attention and trying to hold us where we were until his infantry columns could come up. In the afternoon, probably 2:30 or a little later, a heavy force of the enemy's cavalry made a charge on a battalion of Confederate artillery in advance of us on the same road. To check this cavalry charge, we were hurried across Sailor's Creek, reaching the guns of Colonel Huger's battalion in time to see most of the artillerists, including Colonel Huger, taken away as prisoners. The enemy not being able to take these guns away, as we were now at their heels, they hurriedly chopped with an axe the spokes out of the wheels, disabling them for present use, then retreated, we following in line of battle and going forward through an open field, meeting no resistance, and halting on a piece of high ground. A squadron of Federal cavalry, spying General Pickett with his staff riding up in our rear, made a dash for him; about the same time he discovered the object of these bold riders, and galloped quickly to the lines of the brigade to our left, which was in a body of scattering timber. These reckless troopers pushed up after the General until close to our men, who fired upon them, emptying every saddle. This incident is given to show the reader how desperate was this prolonged game of death.

On the brow of the hill where our brigade halted on the road on which we had been marching, there was intersection with another road leading directly west. Here we hurriedly tore away an old worm fence, piling up the rails to make some protection against rifle balls. On the left rear of Pickett's and part of Bushrod Johnson's divisions on Sailor's Creek were Custis Lee's and Kershaw's 3000 men under General Ewell, with whom we had no connection, nor with Mahone's division and other troops ahead of us, leaving gaps through which the Federal cavalry passed, enabling them to get on our flanks and rear. The enemy's troops in this engagement—one army corps with three cavalry divisions—numbered 25,000 or more men, while the Confederates did not have 7500 all told. The fighting was desperate. Along our front and fully five hundred yards away we could see passing to our right heavy bodies of the enemy, evidently bent upon getting ahead of us. Moreover, this must have been manifest to our commanding officers, who permitted us to remain idle for several hours and until the enemy made full preparations to attack us. That somebody blundered, there is no doubt, as any enlisted man in the ranks could clearly see. We should have moved on. The attack came between 3 and 4 o'clock P.M. by an assault on Munford's dismounted cavalry in a skirt of woods to our right. This attack, as were others on our right front, was repulsed.

General Terry, our brigade commander, had given the order to move to the right, when he discovered another advance upon us, this time in heavy force. We were ordered to remain where we were and not to fire until the enemy were close enough to see the whites of their eyes, then fire and charge with the bayonet. We were behind the rails, close to the ground. The enemy, armed with repeating rifles, when within seventy-five yards or so opened upon us, filling the air with balls, and coming at us. Every man who raised his head above the rails gave his life for the venture. Captain Harris, the Adjutant General of the brigade, raised his head to look and fell back dead; a sandy haired man of my regiment at my elbow met the same fate. He was from Orange County and never knew what hit him. Then came a lull in the firing in front, and I heard a noise behind us; looking around, I saw a column of Federal cavalry close behind us, one of whom had boldly dashed up behind our regiment, seized the colors, and with drawn saber compelled Torbett, the color bearer, to surrender the same. Such was the character and bravery of the men we had to fight. Some one just then cried, "Fire!" and a portion of our regiment delivered its fire into the faces of the enemy in front. In a moment began an indiscriminate fight with clubbed muskets, flagstaffs, pistols and sabers. In a few moments all was over. We had met the enemy and we were theirs. This final struggle was most tragic. We were now marched out and surrounded by a cordon of cavalry.

Ewell's, Kershaw's and Custis Lee's battle on the left was still raging, but to terminate, as had ours, in their capture, together with the greater part of their commands, which had made a brave and gallant fight, but like ourselves were the victims of gross blunders on the part of someone in authority on the field, as well as overwhelmed by superior numbers. This battle ended my activities in the army. There remains only to describe my experience as a prisoner of war, which I will do later on.

The Federal losses in this battle were 166 killed, 1014 wounded. The Confederate losses, 268 killed, 2032 wounded, together with some 6000 prisoners claimed by the enemy. A portion of the division escaped with General Pickett and reached Appomattox.

I am unable to give the number of the killed, wounded and captured of our division, brigade or regiment. I do not, however, believe the 7th Virginia in this battle numbered two hundred, the brigade five hundred, the division not exceeding two thousand. Company D had two officers and sixteen men in this battle, having no loss in killed or wounded. Suffice it to say that with our small number we could not have been driven from our position by parallel battle line.

Four years before this company left Pearisburg, Virginia, with 102 men, the majority of whom were as promising and gallant young men as Virginia produced. During the time of service twenty recruits were added, making 122 in all, and now here we were with eighteen left. The reader is left to ask where were the 104. Let the crippled and mangled survivors who had been discharged, the graves of the noble dead scattered all over Virginia, Maryland and Pennsylvania, make answer. Can anyone wonder that we eighteen were drawn together that day by a bond of suffering and blighted hope, closer than ever before?

Here are the names of the men of Company D present in this last tragic struggle, to-wit: Captain R. H. Bane, Lieutenant Thomas S. Taylor; the men, Fry, Yager, Shannon, Bolton, Darr, Eaton, Gordon, Henderson, J. J. Hurt, C. Minnich, G. A. Minnich, Suthern, Stafford, Wiley, Meadows and the writer.

Strange were the scenes among the captives at Sailor's Creek: some cried, some prayed, others were angry; some cursed, abusing the one who blundered, leading us into the trap to be captured, while a few were cheerful, saying all is not yet lost, but it was apparent to the writer that we had fired our last gun. The flag we had followed to victory on so many fields was now furled forever, and strong men wept!

The sun was fast sinking; the men lay down upon the ground and were soon asleep, many not waking until the sun was high in the heavens the next day. Gloom was depicted on every countenance, and sorrow was in every face. These men had seen their comrades go down day by day, by which they were impressed that if the war continued it was only a question of time when they too would bite the dust. They, however, had this consolation regarding their fallen comrades: that they had gone down in the conscientious belief in the justness of their cause, in the hope of victory, and had not lived to see their flag furled in defeat, and were saved the humiliation of tasting the bitter cup of submission, of which we were to drink to its very dregs. Maybe these after all were the lucky men—who knows? The gallantry and devotion of our soldiers in the unequal struggle proved how thorough were their convictions of the righteousness of their cause. Their devotion to that cause and their kindness and humanity to those whom the fate of war placed in their power, proved them worthy sons of noble ancestry. These men viewed the attempt at coercion on the part of the Northern people as aggression, and their action in defense of their country, homes and firesides, as an inherent, inalienable right—a defense of constitutional liberty.

Immediately upon our capture, the Federal soldiers stripped many of our men of all their good hats, boots and small trinkets. Colonel Flowerree, who had a splendid new hat and boots, was deprived of both, and in lieu thereof was given a worn out, dingy old cap and rough shoes. I think they took these things as souvenirs—war trophies—they did not need them, for they were well supplied.

We were without food and had been practically so since the preceding Monday. Our captors themselves were poorly supplied, but our humane, brave and generous foes divided their scanty supply with us. All of the men captured in the battle of the day before, about six thousand, the Federals then claimed, were congregated with us in the field in which we were placed.

CHAPTER XXVIII

- **To Prison at Point Lookout, Maryland.**

- **Prison Life.**

- **Release.**

Near noon on Friday, April 7, the march was taken up for prison at Point Lookout, a distance of about 150 miles, though at that time we did not know our destination. The Federal soldiers were still taking from our men hats and other articles that pleased their fancy. I noted in my description of the battle of Dreury's Bluff that an Irish sergeant of the 1st Virginia regiment had picked up a fine hat on the battlefield which he had given to me because it would not fit his head, but did mine. I kept this hat until the opening of the campaign in March, 1865, when I put it on, believing this would be our last campaign. When captured at Sailor's Creek I was wearing this hat, and on observing the Federal soldiers capturing hats from our men, I kept as far away from them as I could until we began the march on the 7th, when, crossing a pond, I soused my hat in the muddy water, which made it then appear as worthless, but it was safe in my possession. I wore it to prison, then cleaned off the mud and wore it home. This hat, a blanket and a canteen were the only Federal trophies of the war I carried home.

Late in the evening of April 7, while on the march, we met a drove of beef cattle being driven forward for use of the Federal army. We were halted while a number of these beeves were slaughtered, dressed, cut up into small parcels and handed us where we stood in the road, and we marched on without opportunity to cook the beef, which we devoured blood raw, without salt. This probably may shock the reader, but it was the best that could be done.

On the night march of the 7th from Burkeville I could have escaped, but I reasoned that if I did I would most likely be recaptured, and if I was not I would probably starve, as there was no food in the country, so I determined to risk our captors to give us food.

Next morning we were near Nottoway and passed that day through Petersburg, halting on Thursday, the 13th, near 10 o'clock A.M., at the Federal commissary, nearly a mile beyond the city, where a bountiful supply of food was given us—the first we had received since March 29. Several men were too sick to eat, I of the number, enfeebled as we were from our long continued marching and from dysentery, resulting from eating raw, warm beef, without salt. Resuming the march late in the evening, City Point was reached at dark, where we were huddled together, forced to stand all night in mud several inches deep, in a drizzling rain, without rest or sleep, not even a place to sit down, unless in the mud and water. Such is war.

Next day, April 14, we were placed aboard a steamer, that evening dropping down the James River. Next morning, Saturday the 15th, found our vessel anchored off Point Lookout. Here we first heard of Mr. Lincoln's assassination the preceding night, which at first we were not disposed to credit, but were soon convinced that some fearful catastrophe had taken place, as the flags on the shipping were at half mast. As soon as we were landed we became satisfied that the report of Mr. Lincoln's death was true, the Federal soldiers informing us that any signs of exultation would result in the opening of the batteries on us. We saw that the guns were pointed at the prison. They, however, mistook the spirit and feelings of our men, who, though stung by defeat, yet brave and chivalrous foes, they could in no wise justify, excuse or palliate so cold-blooded a murder, much less rejoice at its commission. They regretted greatly the death of Mr. Lincoln, and spoke of him in the tenderest terms, saying had he lived he would have been kind to our people.

As we entered the prison walls, every man was searched and everything of value (which was little) taken from him. The quarters consisted of small tents, large enough for about five men, into which were crowded about eight to ten, divided into companies in charge of our own sergeants.

Around the prison was a high plank fence with a platform at the top, on which the guards made their beats. The water was bad—brackish, discoloring our teeth. The number of Confederates in this prison was more than 23,000 men, covering about twenty-two acres of land—more than 1,000 to the acre. The number of deaths among the prisoners reported was, from April to July, over 6,800. Among these was Josephus Suthern, of Company D, 7th regiment. I found in this prison Sumner, Crawford, Dudley and Mullins, of Company D, who, with those captured at Sailor's Creek, to wit: Fry, Yager, Shannon, Bolton, Darr, Eaton, Gordon, Henderson, Jim Hurt, Meadows, C. Minnich, George A. Minnich, Suthern, Stafford, Wiley and the writer, making the number twenty in prison. When we met under these new conditions, strange sensations were experienced, as the reader may well suppose.

The only place we were allowed to go outside of the prison, and that only in the daytime, was on the Chesapeake bayside. Our rations consisted of eight ounces of loaf bread per day, a thin piece of bacon or salt pork boiled and cut so thin that it was almost transparent, and a pint cup of bean soup, in which we occasionally found a bean. As a result we were always hungry—went to bed hungry, dreamed of being hungry, and got up ready for breakfast with the same feeling. I went to prison weighing one hundred and sixty-five pounds, not sick a day after I got there, and came out weighing one hundred and twenty-seven pounds. Carrying out the ratio, if I had stayed there six months I would have weighed nothing. We were constantly in danger of being wounded or losing our lives by the reckless firing of the negro guards into the prison at some one claimed by them to be violating the prison rules. We had nothing to read except now and then when we found some man with a Bible or Testament. Some of the men were ingenious workmen, making rings from gutta percha buttons and selling them to the guards.

Near the middle of June orders came for the discharge of the prisoners, upon taking the oath of fidelity to the United States. The men were to be taken out in alphabetical order and transported away as rapidly as could be done. As soon as it was announced that men's names beginning with the letter A would repair to headquarters, then it seemed to all appearances that half the prisoners had names beginning with the letter A. Many a poor fellow, in his anxiety to get away, went out under an assumed name. The letter J was called on Wednesday, June 28, when the numbers in the prison had been greatly reduced, though only the ninth letter of the alphabet had been passed.

Repairing to headquarters, thirty-two fell into line under the American flag unfolded over their heads and had the oath administered to them; the officers taking a personal description of each man, furnishing him the oath and certificate of discharge in writing, when he was passed outside the prison wall. Here follows an exact copy of the oath taken by me and certificate of discharge from prison:

UNITED STATES OF AMERICA.

I, David E. Johnston, of the County of Giles and State of Va., do solemnly swear that I will support, protect and defend the Constitution and Government of the United States against all enemies, whether domestic or foreign; that I will bear true faith, allegiance and loyalty to the same, any ordinance, resolution, or laws of any state, convention or legislature to the contrary notwithstanding; and further, that I will faithfully perform all the duties which may be required of me by the laws of the United States; and that I take this oath freely and voluntarily without any mental reservation or evasion whatever.

(Signed) D. E. JOHNSTON.

Subscribed and sworn to before me this 28th day of June, A.D. 1865.

(Signed) A. C. BRADY,
Maj. and Provost Marshal.

The above named has fair complexion, brown hair and hazel eyes, and is 5 feet 9½ inches high.

CERTIFICATE OF RELEASE OF PRISONER OF WAR.

Headquarters, Point Lookout, Md.

Provost Marshal's Office, June 28, 1865.

I hereby certify that David E. Johnston, prisoner of war, having this day taken the Oath of Allegiance to the United States, is, in conformity with instructions from the War Department, hereby released and discharged. In Witness Whereof I hereunto affix my official signature and stamp.

(Signed) A. C. BRADY,
Maj. and Provost Marshal.

A. C. BRADY,
June 28, 1865.
Maj. and Provost Marshal.

The reader may be interested to know that I have grown a full inch in height and gained more than 80 pounds in weight.

Steamers were at the wharf and as soon as it was known that a sufficient number of those whose destination was Richmond were discharged to load the vessel, we went aboard, landing at Richmond the evening of June 29, and walked up on to the streets, which for the most part were deserted, the city in ruins.

This was Richmond, on the majestic James—the proudest city of Virginia, for whose capture great armies had contended for nearly four years; not only the capital of Virginia, but of the Confederacy, doing more for the Confederate soldier than any other place in the South. Her people were intelligent and high minded and patriotic. I had seen her in her power and glory, but now in the ashes of her destruction, poverty and humiliation. I have since seen her in her opulence and more than her former greatness and glory.

On landing we found ourselves among a people as poor and destitute as we. With no money, no food, no place to stay, traveling without scrip or purse, we finally made our way to old Chimborazo Hospital, where we slept that night on the grass in the yard. The next morning early we made our way to the Danville depot, where a crowd of several hundred ex-Confederate soldiers were congregated, trying to get some kind of transportation home. An old, broken down engine was found by some one in the shop and some box cars in the yard, which were cobbled on, making up a train sufficient, by close packing inside the boxes and on top, to bear the crowd away. I, with others, concluded to try the top of a box car, as we would have more room and plenty of air, but the car, being covered with metal, the heat up there from both the sun and the metal on the car made it no very comfortable place. The engine, too cranky to do much pulling, stuck on the first grade, but after much labor it started again, making slow progress. Late in the evening we had a severe electric storm, accompanied by a heavy downpour of rain, giving those on the boxes a thorough drenching. Those of us going to Lynchburg left the train at Burkeville to make Farmville, which we did in time to catch another train of box cars which carried us to within six miles of Lynchburg, where we boarded a packet boat, getting into Lynchburg late in the evening. There we found quarters in a building called the "Soldiers' Home." We had little to eat that night, but more the next day, Sunday, having to remain over till Monday morning for a train that would carry us westward over the Virginia and Tennessee Railroad. Leaving on Monday morning, we reached Big Spring at the foot of the Alleghanies, where the railroad was again broken. By this time our numbers had been reduced to three—Leonard, of Carroll; Sam Lucas, of Giles, and the writer. We now trudged along afoot till we passed through Alleghany tunnel, where Lucas left us, turning to the right for his home. Leonard and I tramped on, dark overtaking us at Christiansburg depot, where, hungry and worn out, we sought the shades of a friendly oak and, with nothing to eat, lay down and went to sleep.

Our tramp was resumed early on Tuesday, July 4. After a mile or so, finding ourselves growing weaker and our hunger increasing, we then for the first time decided to beg, and succeeded in getting some bread and our canteens filled with milk, which we finished on the spot. Moving on, we crossed New River, on the partially destroyed railroad bridge, beyond which a mile or so we received another supply of milk. On reaching Dublin, my comrade and friend, Leonard, bidding me goodbye, took the left hand and I the right. I was now heading directly for home, and after walking about two and a half miles, it being about 2 P.M., I decided to sit down and rest. I propped myself against a small oak sapling by the roadside, and when I awoke the sun was behind the western mountains. Eight miles further on I reached the home of Mr. Thomas Shannon, who kindly took me in, fed me and gave me a bed. About 3 P.M. on the next day, Wednesday, July 5, 1865, four years, one month and twelve days from the day on which I had left for the war, I reached home—satisfied with my experience, with no more desire for war, yet proud of my record as a Confederate soldier, as I am to this day; with no apologies to make to anyone, as I, in common with my fellow soldiers, repudiate as unsound and baseless any charge of rebellion or treason in the war. We had resorted to the revolutionary right to establish separate government vouchsafed to us in the Declaration of Independence. I did not fight to destroy the government of the United States, nor for the perpetuation of the institution of slavery, for which I cared nothing, but did fight for four years of my young manhood for a principle I knew to be right. Had such not been true, I would not have risked my life, my all, therefor, nor have been a Virginia Confederate soldier.

I doubt not, had the South at any time during the contest agreed to return to the Union, that the Federal soldier would have thrown down his musket and gone home, for he was not fighting for the destruction of slavery, but for the preservation and restoration of the Union. I attach no blame to the brave Union soldier. He was as sincere and conscientious in the fight he made as was I in the one I made. We were both right from our respective viewpoints. With charity for all and malice towards none, this narrative is closed.

CHAPTER XXIX

- **The Conclusion.**

- **War Ends.**

- **The Return to Civil Pursuits.**

- **The Confederate Soldier.**

The war was now ended, the issues involved settled and closed, so far as they could be by the sword. The Federal government had stood the test, proved itself too strong for the allied seceded states, overthrown their separate government, maintained by a separate people for four years, and established the fact that no state could secede or leave the Union unless by revolution and force of arms strong enough to defy and successfully resist the power of the general government. Slavery was abolished and could not exist among the American people. To accomplish these two things had cost thousands of lives, anguish, blood and billions of treasure.

With the close of the war the survivors of Company D who were either at home or in hospital when the war ended, or who had gotten home from the surrender at Appomattox, or had been released from military prisons, accepted the result of the conflict in good faith and again entered the pursuits of civil life. As they had been gallant soldiers, they became law-abiding, upright and worthy citizens. Numbers of the company had perished on the battlefield, in hospitals and in prison. Some were buried on the field where they fell, with no monument or slab to mark their last resting place, yet they died for a cause the justness of which they never for a moment doubted. The survivors lived to see their efforts for separate government defeated, the principles and the righteousness of the cause not lost, but the struggle to establish and maintain the same had failed. This failure is, however, no argument against the justness and right of the cause. No braver, nobler company of men had part in the contest than the company of which I write. Theirs was a sacrifice for liberty not to be gained and a struggle in which all was lost save honor and manhood.

Now (1914), nearly fifty years have passed since the close of the mighty conflict, and there remain alive of those brave men who stood on the firing line, baring their bosoms to the storm, but few, eighteen, so far as I know or can ascertain, and whose names are as follows: A. L. Fry, J. T. Frazier, John A. Hale, B. L. Hoge, James J. Hurt, David E. Johnston, —— Lewy, N. J. Morris, Thomas N. Mustain, A. C. Pack, William D. Peters, John W.

Sarver, Alexander Skeens, Joseph Skeens, W. H. H. Snidow, Thomas J. Stafford, Gordon L. Wilburn and Jesse B. Young.

In what is said herein in praise of the honor and glory won in war and peace by the Confederate soldier, particularly of those of the Army of Northern Virginia, with which I served throughout the four years' struggle, I do not for one moment mean or intend to detract from the laurels won by the heroic Union soldier, who stood in the firing line, faithfully discharging his duty; for he, as well as we, was contending for principles regarded sacred and for which we had risked our lives, and in which struggle one or the other of the combatants must yield. All were American soldiers, and the glory and honor won by each is the common heritage of the American people, not to be obscured or clouded by the questions about which we differed. Each struggled to maintain the right as God gave him to see the right.

We often talked along the skirmish lines with Union soldiers and they invariably and vehemently denied that they were fighting to abolish or destroy slavery. Particularly was this true of those from the Northwestern states. In opposition to our claim or contention that we were fighting for independence—separate government—they insisted that they were fighting for the Union, a common, undivided country; did not want to see the country broken up by division; and I feel fairly safe in stating that this feeling and sentiment largely dominated the great majority of the Union soldiers. I recall one or more conversations with Union soldiers along the lines on the above subject, in which they told me that if they believed they were fighting to free the slaves they would quit the army and go home.

The Confederate soldier, as I have already said, accepted in good faith the result of the war, bore no malice toward those whom he had fought face to face, knowing:

"Malice is a wrinkled hag, hell-born;

Her heart is hate, her soul is scorn.

Blinded with blood, she cannot see

To do any deed of charity."

And again remembering the thought expressed in the lines:

"You cannot tame the tiger,

   You dare not kill the dove;

But every gate you bar with hate

Will open wide to love."

No such army ever trod this earth as the Army of Northern Virginia, composed of the best body of fighting men that ever shouldered a musket. President Roosevelt said of them: "The world has never seen better soldiers than those who followed Lee."

The Federal General Hooker—"Fighting Joe," as he was aptly called by his soldiers, in his testimony before the committee of Congress on the conduct of the war, in speaking of the Army of Northern Virginia, among other things said: "That army had by discipline alone a character for steadiness and efficiency unsurpassed, in my judgment, in ancient or modern times. We have not been able to rival it."

Colonel David F. Pugh, a gallant Federal soldier, and a late commander of the Grand Army of the Republic, in an address delivered by him at the unveiling of the Confederate monument at Camp Chase, Ohio, June 7, 1902, said: "All the bitterness has gone out of my heart, and in spite of a Confederate bullet in my body, I do not hesitate to acknowledge that their valor is part of the common heritage of the whole country. We can never challenge the fame of those men whose skill and valor made them the idols of the Confederate army. The fame of Lee, Jackson, the Johnstons, Gordon, Longstreet, the Hills, Hood and Stuart and many thousands of non-commissioned officers and private soldiers of the Confederate armies, whose names are not mentioned on historic pages, can never be tarnished by the carping criticisms of the narrow and shallow minded."

If this be the estimate of a Northern president and of a leading general of our adversaries, who at one time commanded the gallant Army of the Potomac, and of the other brave Federal soldier whom I have quoted, what shall we in truth say for ourselves?

Lieutenant-General Early, among the bravest and best soldiers in the Army of Northern Virginia, and who fought nearly a hundred battles and skirmishes, hence competent to speak on the subject, in his Memoirs says: "I believe the world has never produced a body of men superior in courage, patriotism and endurance to the private soldiers of the Confederate armies. I have repeatedly, seen these soldiers submit with cheerfulness to privations and hardships which would appear to be almost incredible; and the wild cheers of our brave men, when their lines sent back opposing hosts of Federal troops, staggering, reeling and flying, have often thrilled every fiber in my heart. I have seen with my own eyes ragged, barefooted and hungry Confederate soldiers perform deeds which, if performed in days of yore by mailed warriors in glittering armor, would have inspired the harp of the minstrel and the pen of the poet."

But arguing the nobility of the Confederate soldier is like arguing the brightness of the sun at noonday. The Confederate soldier was truly an American, for his people in the South were the truest type of Americans in the land, having very little foreign population among them. Again, this Confederate soldier was born and reared a gentleman, was so by instinct. He was not a mercenary; he was neither for conquest nor aggression, but stood purely for self-defense. He believed in his inmost soul that no people had juster cause, higher aspirations, or made braver or nobler resolves for cause, country, families, homes and firesides. I turn to ask, who were these Confederate soldiers? They were principally country folks, farmers, mechanics, school boys, as stated; native born Americans, descendants of Revolutionary patriots, by no means all slave owners; thousands never owned slaves, and many were opposed to the institution. The Confederate soldier was always impatient of military restraint, feeling himself the equal of and as good as any man, and not inferior to his superior in rank; in battle, as a rule, his own general; his individuality and self-reliance, among his noted characteristics, were the crowning glory of his actions, and this self-reliance taught him when it was wise and prudent to fight, and when it was the better part of valor to decline. On the battlefield he was at his best; "his clothes might be ragged, but his musket and saber were bright. His haversack empty, but he kept his cartridge box filled. Often his feet were bare, blistered and bleeding; occasionally he might straggle on the march, but was up when the battle was on."

Barefoot, ragged, without food, no pay and nothing to buy if he had money, he marched further, laughed louder, making the welkin ring with his rebel yell; endured more genuine suffering, hardship and fatigue, fought more bravely, complained and fretted less, than any soldier who marched beneath the banners of Napoleon. His nerve was steady and his aim was sure, and his powers of endurance and resistance unmeasured. This same Confederate soldier fought and hoped and hoped and fought:

"Sometimes he won, then hopes were high;

Again he lost, but it would not die;

And so to the end he followed and fought,

With love and devotion, which could not be bought."

Though his ears were often greeted with the cries of woe and distress of those at home (enough to break his heart), his ardor chilled not; he had a never faltering courage; his spirit remained unbroken, his convictions never yielded. In the darkest hour of our peril, in the midst of dark and lowering clouds, with scarcely the glimmer of a star of apparent hope, he still stood firm and grasped his musket with a tighter grip. Following is the description given of this soldier by another:

"Look at the picture of this soldier as he stood in the iron and leaden hail, with his old, worn out slouch hat, his bright eyes glistening with excitement, powder-begrimed face, rent and ragged clothing, with the prints of his bare feet in the dust of the battle, a genuine tatterdemalion, fighting bravely, with no hope of reward, promotion or pay, with little to eat and that often cornbread and sorghum molasses. If he stopped a Yankee bullet and was thereby killed, he was buried on the field and forgotten, except by comrades or a loving old mother at home."

"In the solemn shades of the wood that swept

    The field where his comrades found him,

They buried him there—and the big tears crept

    Into strong men's eyes that had seldom wept.

His mother—God pity her!—smiled and slept,

    Dreaming her arms were around him."

In modern times there has never been such valor and heroism displayed as in our Civil War, never such soldiers as the Union and Confederate, and certainly never such as the Confederate soldiers, and it would be nothing to their credit to have achieved victories over less valorous foes than the Union soldiers, and no credit to the Union soldiers that they overwhelmed men of less bravery. The individuality of the Confederate soldier was never lost, and this with his self-possession and intelligent thought made him well nigh invincible. The Army of Northern Virginia as a whole was never driven from a battlefield, although confronted by as good soldiers as were on the continent. No danger could appall these men of Lee, no peril awe, no hardships dismay, no numbers intimidate. To them duty was an inspiration. They had devastated no fields, desecrated no temples and plundered no people, always respecting woman, and feared no man. The record of these soldiers since the war is clean, their names a stranger to criminal records; few, if any, who followed Lee have been behind the bars of a jail. He was their great exemplar. Thousands of these non-commissioned officers and private soldiers, after the first year of the war, were fitted not only to command regiments, but could well have filled much higher military positions.

Great soldiers were Lee, Johnston, Jackson, Longstreet, Hills, Pickett, Stuart and others, but who made them great? No generals ever had such soldiers. It was these Confederates in the ranks that made the names of their generals immortal. Who would have ever heard of them, or of General Grant, but for the Confederate soldier?

What this Confederate soldier has been to the South since the war cannot be measured or stated. Shortly after the close of the conflict and he had reached his home, if he had one left, his troubles were not over. He was confronted with the aftermath—the carpet-bagger and the scallawag, as well as by military-enforced reconstruction, the blackest spot on the page of American history. Well we might and did forgive the wrongs of war, but how were we to overlook and forget the outrageous and shameful things done in the name of restoration of civil government, by the carpetbagger, Northern political pest and pirate—the Southern scallawag, the low, mean, unworthy Southern white man, thrown to the surface by the revolution, but, like all dirt and filth, to go to the bottom and sink in the mud when the flood had subsided.

Serious and grave as these questions were, which sorely tried the Confederate soldier's courage, patience and forbearance, as they had been tested in war, he met them bravely, firmly and by his indomitable spirit directed and controlled them. His broad, keen, intelligent knowledge of men and things finally carried him through the trying ordeal, and crowned his labors with stable governments for the states of his Southland, the most American conservative portion of the republic, made so largely by the brain, brawn, energy and industry of the Confederate soldier, who has been the leader, promoter and architect of her industrial and political fortunes, the idol of her people, her representative in the every fiber and thought of her existence and governments. He has raised her from her ashes and poverty into a veritable garden and to industrial and political power. The last roll call will shortly be sounded, his sun will soon set—what a hero! What an object of interest, will be the last surviving soldier of the Confederacy (I crave to be the one!), the only and last representative of that government of which the great English scholar and poet, Professor Worsely, has written:

"No nation ever rose so white and fair,

Or fell so free of crime."

APPENDIX NO. 1

RANK, WOUNDS, DEATHS, DISCHARGES, ETC.

No. 1. James H. French, captain first year of war; led the company in battles of Bull Run and First Manassas.

No. 2. Eustace Gibson, first lieutenant first year of war; in battles Bull Run and First Manassas. Brave soldier.

No. 3. W. A. Anderson, second lieutenant first year.

No. 4. Joel Blackard, second junior lieutenant first year; elected captain at reorganization, April, 1862; in battles of Bull Run, First Manassas, Williamsburg, Seven Pines, Cold Harbor; killed in Battle of Frazier's Farm, June 30, 1862.

No. 5. R. H. Bane, sergeant; elected first lieutenant at reorganization, April, 1862; promoted captain on death of Blackard; wounded at First Battle of Manassas; led the company for the remainder of the war; died since the war.

No. 6. John W. Mullins, second sergeant; promoted to first sergeant; elected second lieutenant at reorganization, April, 1862; wounded at Second Battle of Manassas and Howlett House, dying of wound received at last named place.

No. 7. Elisha M. Stone, corporal; elected third lieutenant at reorganization, April, 1862; wounded in battles of Williamsburg and Gettysburg; captured at last named battle; remained a prisoner to close of the war; led Company E, 7th regiment, in Battle of Gettysburg.

No. 8. Elijah R. Walker, elected second junior lieutenant in 1862; promoted to second lieutenant on death of Mullins; wounded in battles of Seven Pines and Gettysburg; disabled for service in last named battle, and retired in April, 1864.

No. 9. Thomas S. Taylor, first sergeant; elected second lieutenant, November 25, 1864; slightly wounded at Gettysburg; captured at Battle of Sailor's Creek.

No. 10. A. C. Pack, first sergeant; in battles of Bull Run and First Manassas; discharged on account of disability in Fall of 1861.

No. 11. B. P. Watts, elected second sergeant, but on account of ill health not mustered into service.

No. 12. J. C. Hughes, elected third sergeant in April, 1861; in prison at close of war.

No. 13. William D. Peters, fourth sergeant in April, 1861; third sergeant at reorganization; severely wounded at Battle of Five Forks, April 1, 1865.

No. 14. Hamilton J. Hale, fifth sergeant; died at Culpeper, October, 1861.

No. 15. A. L. Fry, first sergeant; wounded at First Battle of Manassas; captured at Warrenton, September, 1862; slightly wounded at Battle of Plymouth, N.C., April, 1864; captured at Battle of Sailor's Creek, April, 1865; a prisoner at Point Lookout at close of the war.

No. 16. W. H. H. Snidow, second sergeant; in Confederate prison at close of the war.

No. 17. Joseph C. Shannon, fourth sergeant; slightly wounded at Battle of Frazier's Farm; captured at Battle of Sailor's Creek; a prisoner at Point Lookout.

No. 18. David E. Johnston, fourth sergeant; slightly wounded at Battle of Williamsburg; appointed sergeant-major 7th Virginia Regiment, December 10, 1862; severely wounded at Battle of Gettysburg, July 3, 1863; left on the field and captured; also captured at Battle of Sailor's Creek, April 6, 1865; a prisoner at Point Lookout at end of the war.

No. 19. T. N. Mustain, second corporal; transferred 1862 to 57th Virginia Infantry.

No. 20. John W. Hight, fourth corporal; wounded at battles of Seven Pines and Second Manassas; captured at Gettysburg on third day's battle; deserted.

No. 21. A. J. Thompson, first corporal; wounded at Battle of Williamsburg; in prison at close of war. No better soldier.

No. 22. Daniel Bish, second corporal; wounded at Battle of Frazier's Farm; killed at Battle of Gettysburg, third day.

No. 23. George C. Mullins, third corporal; captured at Battle of Five Forks; a prisoner at Point Lookout.

No. 24. Jesse B. Young, fourth corporal; temporary regimental ensign; wounded at battles of Frazier's Farm and Gettysburg and captured; again wounded in Battle at Clay's House. A brave and valiant soldier.

No. 25. Edward Z. Yager, first sergeant in 1864; wounded in Battle of Williamsburg; captured at Sailor's Creek; prisoner at Point Lookout.

No. 26. David C. Akers, wounded at Battle of Frazier's Farm; killed in Battle of Gettysburg.

No. 27. George W. Akers, died in 1862.

No. 28. W. R. Albert, discharged in 1862.

No. 29. Allen M. Bane, transferred from 4th Virginia regiment in exchange for John H. Martin, of Company D; wounded in Battle of Williamsburg; captured at Battle of Frazier's Farm; transferred to 1st Kentucky battalion of cavalry.

No. 30. Alexander Bolton, cook and member of ambulance corps; a prisoner at Point Lookout.

No. 31. Joseph E. Bane, killed at First Battle of Manassas.

No. 32. Jesse Barrett, killed at Battle of Gettysburg, third day.

No. 33. Travis Burton, wounded at Battle of Seven Pines; transferred.

No. 34. W. H. Carr, wounded at Second Battle of Manassas; retired.

No. 35. James M. Collins, detailed as blacksmith.

No. 36. John R. Crawford, slightly wounded at Battle of Boonsboro Gap; captured in Battle of Five Forks; a prisoner at Point Lookout.

No. 37. William Crawford, over age; discharged.

No. 38. James B. Croy, on special service; captured and held a prisoner until near end of war.

No. 39. James Cole, killed at Battle of Boonsboro Gap.

No. 40. T. P. Darr, wounded and taken prisoner at Battle of Frazier's Farm; captured at Battle of Sailor's Creek; a prisoner at Point Lookout.

No. 41. John S. Dudley, wounded in Second Battle of Manassas; also at Sharpsburg, and captured; slightly wounded at Dreury's Bluff; captured at Five Forks; a prisoner at Point Lookout.

No. 42. M. J. Dulaney, died June, 1862.

No. 43. D. R. Dulaney, transferred to Virginia Reserves.

No. 44. W. H. Douthat, discharged in 1862.

No. 45. Thomas Davenport, deserted in Spring, 1862.

No. 46. David Davis, discharged in 1862.

No. 47. Elbert S. Eaton, wounded in Second Battle of Manassas; captured in Battle of Sailor's Creek; a prisoner at Point Lookout.

No. 48. Elisha D. East, whipped out of service.

No. 49. John W. East, wounded in battles of Williamsburg, Plymouth, N.C., and Dreury's Bluff; deserted in 1864.

No. 50. Joseph A. Eggleston, died in 1862 of wounds received in battle of Frazier's Farm.

No. 51. James H. Eggleston, died of disease, June, 1862.

No. 52. John S. W. French, deserted at Suffolk, Va., May, 1863.

No. 53. F. H. Farley, wounded in second battle of Manassas; deserted in 1864.

No. 54. William C. Fortner, wounded in battle of second Manassas; also at Gettysburg, where he was captured.

No. 55. James H. Fortner, wounded in second battle of Manassas and Gettysburg; left on the field and captured.

No. 56. J. Tyler Frazier; slightly wounded in second battle of Manassas; captured on retreat from Petersburg, 1865.

No. 57. William Frazier, died October, 1861.

No. 58. Creed D. Frazier, discharged in fall 1861.

No. 59. W. A. French, in battles of Bull Run and first Manassas; discharged July, 1861.

No. 60. Andrew J. French, discharged in fall of 1861.

No. 61. James H. Gardner, slightly wounded in battle of Bull Run, July 18, 1861; deserted May, 1863.

No. 62. Francis M. Gordon, wounded in battle of Frazier's Farm; captured in battle of Sailor's Creek; prisoner at Point Lookout.

No. 63. Andrew J. Grigsby, promoted to Major 27th Virginia regiment.

No. 64. Charles A. Hale, surrendered at Appomattox.

No. 65. John A. Hale, wounded in battles of Williamsburg and Five Forks.

No. 66. John D. Hare, died November 23, 1861.

No. 67. Isaac Hare, slightly wounded in battle of Bull Run, and severely wounded in battle of Williamsburg; transferred.

No. 68. John R. Henderson, died October, 1861.

No. 69. James B. Henderson, captured in battle of Sailor's Creek; in prison at Point Lookout.

No. 70. B. L. Hoge, at home sick at close of the war.

No. 71. James Hughes, discharged, died in 1861.

No. 72. James J. Hurt, wounded in battle of Gettysburg; captured at Sailor's Creek, and prisoner at end of the war.

No. 73. George W. Hurt, detached as teamster.

No. 74. John F. Jones, wounded in battle of Gettysburg; leg amputated; discharged.

No. 75. George Johnston, discharged.

No. 76. Manilius S. Johnston, wounded in first battle of Manassas; discharged.

No. 77. George Knoll, wounded in battles of Williamsburg and Boonsboro; captured at last named battle.

No. 78. Charles N. J. Lee, wounded in first battle of Manassas; discharged.

No. 79. Henry Lewey, wounded in first battle of Manassas; surrendered at Appomattox.

No. 80. Joseph Lewey, wounded at battle of Seven Pines; surrendered at Appomattox.

No. 81. W. H. Layton, deserted, February, 1862.

No. 82. James Lindsey, discharged, 1861.

No. 83. P. H. Lefler, discharged in 1862.

No. 84. Anderson Meadows, wounded in battle of Williamsburg; captured at Sailor's Creek; prisoner at Point Lookout.

No. 85. John Meadows, wounded in battles of Williamsburg and Gettysburg; died in 1864.

No. 86. Ballard P. Meadows, died June 18, 1862, of wounds received in battle of Frazier's Farm.

No. 87. N. J. Morris, discharged in 1862.

No. 88. George A. Minnich, wounded in battle of Frazier's Farm; captured in battle of Sailor's Creek; prisoner at Point Lookout.

No. 89. Christian Minnich, captured in battle of Sailor's Creek; prisoner at Point Lookout.

No. 90. John H. Minnich, discharged in 1861.

No. 91. A. D. Manning, killed in battle of Seven Pines.

No. 92. Raleigh Merricks, detailed as teamster.

No. 93. T. P. Mays, wounded in battle of Frazier's Farm; killed in battle of Boonsboro.

No. 94. John H. Martin, transferred in 1861 to 4th Virginia regiment in exchange for Allen M. Bane, transferred to Company D from 4th Virginia regiment.

No. 95. John Q. Martin, killed in second battle of Manassas.

No. 96. W. W. Muncey, wounded in battle of Gettysburg.

No. 97. James J. Nye, died of wounds received in second battle of Manassas.

No. 98. John Palmer, deserted in spring of 1862.

No. 99. Charles W. Peck, Second Corporal, wounded in battle of Williamsburg; died in summer of 1862.

No. 100. John W. Sarver, severely wounded in battle of Frazier's Farm; disabled and discharged.

> No. 101. Demarcus L. Sarver, wounded in battles of Williamsburg and Gettysburg; deserted.

No. 102. Josephus Suthern, wounded in battle of Frazier's Farm; captured in battle of Sailor's Creek; died in prison at Point Lookout.

No. 103. Samuel B. Shannon, wounded in battle of first Manassas; served his one year enlistment; joined 1st Kentucky battalion of cavalry.

No. 104. John P. Sublett, wounded in first battle of Manassas; killed in battle of Gettysburg.

No. 105. William T. Sublett, died October, 1861.

No. 106. Alexander Skeens, discharged in 1862.

No. 107. Joseph Skeens, discharged in 1862.

No. 108. Lewis R. Skeens, died August 6, 1862.

No. 109. A. L. Sumner, captured in battle of Five Forks; prisoner in Point Lookout.

No. 110. Thomas J. Stafford, discharged in 1862.

No. 111. William H. Stafford, killed in battle of Williamsburg.

No. 112. R. M. Stafford, captured in battle of Sailor's Creek; a prisoner in Point Lookout.

No. 113. Adam Thompson, wounded in battle of second Manassas; deserted February, 1864.

No. 114. Alonzo Thompson, died, November, 1862.

No. 115. Lee E. Vass, died August 4, 1862, of wounds received in battle of Frazier's Farm.

No. 116. W. R. C. Vass, killed in second battle of Manassas.

No. 117. Gordon L. Wilburn, wounded in second battle of Manassas; surrendered at Appomattox.

No. 118. Hugh J. Wilburn, wounded in battles of Frazier's Farm and second Manassas; deserted in May, 1863.

No. 119. William I. Wilburn, wounded in battles of Williamsburg, and second Manassas; surrendered at Appomattox.

No. 120. Lewis N. Wiley, wounded in battle of Fredericksburg; captured in battle of Sailor's Creek; a prisoner at Point Lookout.

No. 121. Isaac Young, transferred to 28th Virginia battalion.

No. 122. Thomas J. Young, deserted in February, 1862.

Total Enlistment, 122.

Number killed in battle and died of wounds	17
Number died of disease	14
Number discharged for various causes	29
Number transferred to other commands	6
Number in prison at Point Lookout and other places (at close of war)	27
Number absent, sick in hospital, wounded, or at home (at close of war)	8

Number surrendered at Appomattox	9
Number deserted	12
	122

Memo.—Absent, sick and wounded or at home at close of war:

B. L. Hoge.	George Knoll.
W. W. Munsey.	J. B. Young.
W. C. Fortner.	W. D. Peters.
James H. Fortner.	John A. Hale.

APPENDIX NO. 2

In concluding my reminiscences I have determined to add some statistics as to the campaigns, strength and losses of the two greatest armies of the war—the Army of Northern Virginia and the Federal Army of the Potomac. Never before in modern warfare had it fallen to the lot of two such armies to fight so many bloody battles, with neither able to obtain any decided advantage over the other. Beginning with the battles around Richmond in the spring of 1862, to the close at Appomattox, these two armies fought many battles through seven great campaigns. The Army of Northern Virginia, under General Lee, numbering at its greatest not exceeding 80,000 men, certainly greatly inferior in numbers to that opposed—badly armed, equipped and fed, fought against six most distinguished Federal commanders, to-wit:

- McClellan before Richmond.

- Pope, Cedar Mountain and Manassas.

- McClellan in Maryland.

- Burnside at Fredericksburg.

- Hooker at Chancellorsville.

- Meade at Gettysburg.

- Grant from the Rapidan to Appomattox.

In these campaigns the Federals lost in the aggregate about 263,000 men. The Confederate loss is not definitely known.

General Grant's casualties were about 124,390 men, and in his campaign from March 29, 1865, to April 9, 1865, his losses were 9944.

General Lee's surrender at Appomattox embraced 28,356 men, of whom only 8000 had arms, the residue being largely made up of broken down, barefoot and sick men, teamsters and attaches of the medical, ordnance, quartermaster, and commissary departments.

It may be of interest to the reader to know the number of men enrolled in the Union and the Confederate armies during the war, and the losses in killed, wounded, and prisoners held by each.

Official compilation shows that there were enrolled of white troops in the Union army	2,494,592
Negro troops	<u>178,975</u>
Total	2,673,567
Of this number the white troops from the Southern and border states	278,923
Negro troops	<u>140,298</u>
	419,221
The enrollment of Confederate troops, estimated	700,000

This may not be entirely correct, but is believed to be substantially so.

The Union losses in killed, died from wounds, disease, and from other causes	360,212
Of which the killed in action were	67,058
Died of wounds received in action	43,012
Died of disease	224,586
Deaths from	<u>25,556</u>

other causes, or
from causes
unknown

| Total | 360,212 |

The Confederate losses, as far as
can be ascertained, though not
believed to be entirely correct,
were as follows:

Killed in action	52,954
Died of wounds	21,570
Died of disease	_59,297_
Total	133,821

The number of Confederate prisoners taken and held by the Federal government during the war was	220,000
Number that died in Northern prisons (12 per cent of the total)	26,000
Number of Union prisoners held by Confederates	270,000
Number that died in Southern prisons (less than 9 per cent)	22,000

Confederate
soldiers paroled,   174,223
1865

Number of battles and
skirmishes fought during the war,
over two thousand.

NOTE—The most of the above statistics were obtained from "Confederate Military History," edited by General Clement A. Evans, and from "The Century Book of Facts," by Ruoff.

Milton Keynes UK
Ingram Content Group UK Ltd.
UKHW042145281024
450365UK00010B/616